Successful Business Forecasting

Joan Callahan Compton
Stephen B. Compton

LIBERTY HALL
PRESS™

Notices

d-Base III, is a trademark of Ashton-Tate.
GPSS is a trademark for the GENERAL-PURPOSE SIMULATION SYSTEM.
Lotus 1-2-3 is a registered trademark of the Lotus Development Corporation.
Statgraphics Statistical Graphics System is a registered trademark of the Statistical Graphics Corporation, and is marketed exclusively by STSC, Inc.

LIBERTY HALL PRESS books are published by LIBERTY HALL PRESS an imprint of McGraw-Hill, Inc. Its trademark, consisting of the words "LIBERTY HALL PRESS" and the portrayal of Benjamin Franklin, is registered in the United States Patent and Trademark Office.

FIRST EDITION
THIRD PRINTING

Library of Congress Cataloging-in-Publication Data

Compton, Joan Callahan.
Successful business forecasting / by Joan Callahan Compton and Stephen B. Compton.
p. cm.
Includes bibliographical references.
ISBN 0-8306-0207-0
1. Business forecasting—Statistical methods. I. Compton, Stephen B. II. Title.
HD30.27.C65 1989
658.4′0355—dc20   89-12818
                                                                         CIP

For information about other McGraw-Hill materials,
call 1-800-2-MCGRAW in the U.S. In other countries
call your nearest McGraw-Hill office.

Questions regarding the content of this book should be addressed to:

Reader Inquiry Branch
LIBERTY HALL PRESS
Blue Ridge Summit, PA 17294-0850

Vice President and Editorial Director: David J. Conti
Book Editor: Peter D. Sandler
Production: Katherine G. Brown

Contents

This book is dedicated to our children,
Skye and Daniel.

Foreword

In recent years, more jobs in industry, government, and academia have begun to require a basic knowledge of statistics. The techniques and concepts used in all these areas are the same, whether the discipline is engineering, education, agriculture, psychology, business, biology, medicine, or ecology. A motivating force behind the study of forecasting (or mathematical statistics of any kind) is the likelihood that these principles and methods will at some time be employed in the decision-making process. The ability to function and compete in the modern world requires an understanding of the basic statistical tools; we are becoming increasingly dependent on quantitative information.

The Comptons' book is not limited to business forecasting, but offers professionals in all these fields a common body of knowledge. It is for this reason that I find the treatment in this book to be so insightful. It is not slanted to any particular discipline, but touches on diverse areas of interest in many walks of life. The authors have presented the subject of statistical forecasting in an interesting and humorous way so that the time spent absorbing these basic tenets will not appear to be a punitive sentence, but an interesting exercise with a direct correlation to one's field of interest.

The book covers the topics in statistical forecasting presented in most textbooks of its kind. The significant difference that I have found is that the authors provide a treatment that stimulates the individual interest. Instead of addressing mathematical formalism, they constantly appeal to the reader's intuition and basic abilities to reason and understand.

The book differs from less inspired texts by communicating with the readers, rather than lecturing them; presenting material in a relaxed and informal way, without the omission of important concepts; capturing and recapturing the readers' attention with quotations, names, and unexpected similes of a humorous nature; and most importantly providing an intuitive and common-sense approach to developing concepts.

One limitation of most statistical textbooks is that they are limited in scope and give priority to specific statistical topics. This unique book, which deals with that segment of mathematical statistics called forecasting, is structured to provide the student with a clear understanding of the applications and implementation of the subject, before proceeding to the maturations of the mathematics. The student will actually understand why he or she is learning a specific process, and how it applies to forecasting, before attempting any rote memorization of equations.

Most of us in this field have memories of the long hours spent arduously studying differential equations, then being told that there is a much easier way to understand the functions of a curve. This book provides those basic understandings where they belong: before the process and not after. In short, this book is written for the reader, rather than for the statistician. Its major accomplishment is to convince the student that the study of forecasting can be a lively, interesting, and rewarding experience.

Norm Frigon*

---

*Norm Frigon is a manager at the U.S. Navy's Quality Evaluation Activity in Fallbrook, California. This activity is responsible for the analysis of weapons systems reliability, maintainability, availability, and quality. His group performs statistical analysis and modeling to determine the current status of these systems and to forecast service life. Mr. Frigon also is associate director of the University of Arizona Reliability Management Institute, as well as executive vice president of Quantitative Analysis Inc. He has a B.A. in mathematical statistics and a master's degree in quantitative analysis.

Preface

Hundreds of forecasting textbooks are already available in libraries and bookstores. The topic is also covered in many business textbooks and in most statistics books. Unfortunately, from the viewpoint of most users, such textbooks tend to be highly mathematical and somewhat intimidating. Even textbooks that claim to be designed for nontechnical users make slow reading, although they are useful as reference works.

At the other extreme, some large companies have developed their own instructional materials that explain forecasting at an elementary level. These manuals are useful as far as they go, but typically they suffer from the following shortcomings:

- They are limited to a few forecasting methods that the company uses, so they do not provide an adequate overview of the subject matter. New methods are discouraged because they aren't in the manual.

- Such manuals often contain serious errors, because they tend to be written by people who do not really understand forecasting themselves.

- A corporate procedure manual of any type often takes on a life of its own. When questioned, people point to it and shrug. Once the methods and errors become entrenched, they may be nearly impossible to change.

This book is unique in that it aims for the middle ground. More-over, it contains very few mathematical formulas and practice calculations. Chapter 3 explains the most common terms used in statistics, so that you can get it all over with at once—but if you want to skip this chapter, you still can understand most of the rest of the book.

This might sound like a strange way to teach forecasting, but we have found it effective for two reasons:

First, we don't agree that readers always need to see the formulas. We have observed that most managers prefer concepts. In fact, most formulas tell most readers nothing at all—except, perhaps, that math is incomprehensible and that it might be best to abandon quantitative forecasting altogether. And in many organizations, this is exactly what happens. Less precise methods, such as moving averages or the jury of executive opinion, are substituted for regression or adaptive filtering because the calculations appear to be simpler. Someone should tell these people about computers.

Second, we have seen no evidence that readers benefit from performing tedious calculations by hand. Such exercises are based on the theory that students learn by doing. But this premise is valid only if the exercises reflect the kinds of problems that the working professional encounters in *real life*.

In real life, experienced forecasters rarely perform calculations by hand, unless they are using the very simplest methods. Students frequently are turned off by such exercises. They gain the lifelong impression that statistics is a boring subject, when what really bores them is arithmetic.

In a typical textbook, for example, the section on regression would show you Equations 3-4 and 3-5 (chapter 3). It would then ask you to take a list of data values, plot the points, and calculate the position of the regression line. And it would go on to explain that the line described by these values fits the data better than any other line.

This is a true statement. But would you be convinced simply by looking at these formulas? Why should these strange-looking formulas necessarily yield the best regression line? Rather than try to figure this out, it might seem easier just to take a good guess and draw the line by hand. (Many managers give up and do just that.)

It is possible, of course, to explain why these regression formulas work. We had to learn why in school, and we could explain it as well as anyone else. But this isn't the purpose of our book. If you want to read about mathematics, get a math book. What you have here is an applied forecasting book.

In other words: forecasting methodology, like jet airplanes, need not be understood *fully* to be used effectively. Computer programs are now available for less than $100 which can perform regression calculations and other forecasting procedures on large data sets in seconds. If you don't have too much data, even a programmable calculator will suffice. Several models designed for engineers have optional plug-in modules with a variety of statistical programs.

The forecaster need not memorize formulas, perform calculations by hand, or understand linear algebra. He must, however, understand the general purpose and limitations of each procedure. The forecaster also must be able to decipher the computer output in practical terms that can be applied to the everyday concerns of business. He must be able to recognize which procedures and circumstances are likely to require the assistance of a forecasting specialist.

The main purpose of this book is to equip the manager to cope with typical business forecasting situations and methods. The book is also aimed at programmers and others who may find themselves cast in the role of corporate soothsayer. It emphasizes the information that is likely to be needed by the working forecaster who has a limited background in mathematics or statistics.

Chapter 1 tells why forecasting methods are useful.

Chapter 2 discusses the differences between statistics as it is taught in school and forecasting as it is practiced in business, and attempts to bridge the gap between the two.

Chapter 3 is about elementary statistics. It requires no knowledge of mathematics beyond simple arithmetic. If you run across an unfamiliar term later on, you can look it up here or in the glossary.

Chapter 4 defines the basic types of forecasting models, and tells you how to decide which model to use.

Chapters 5 through 7 present the most common forecasting methods in more detail, grouped according to the type of model or concept they represent.

Chapter 8 addresses the important topic of forecast monitoring and revision—that is, how to tell whether your forecasting method is working adequately, and how to take corrective action if it is not.

Chapter 9 discusses the role of computers in forecasting and reviews some useful forecasting software packages.

The Glossary defines over four hundred terms that are commonly used in forecasting. The list is not limited to terms that appear in the book, but also includes expressions borrowed from such diverse fields as mathematics, statistics, marketing, and inventory management.

Finally, the Bibliography lists some forecasting books and articles that you may find useful.

1
Introduction

Don't never prophesy—onless ye know.

—James Russell Lowell

This chapter will introduce you to the following topics:

- The meaning of the term *forecasting*.
- The reasons for forecasting.
- The general qualifications of a successful forecaster.

WHAT IS FORECASTING?

The word *forecasting*, in the popular sense, generally refers to any attempt to predict some future event of interest. All of the following are examples of forecasting:

- A marketing manager tries to project next year's pattern of demand for a given product line, based on past sales.
- A TV network weather commentator studies meteorological data and estimates the probability that it will rain this weekend.
- An economist attempts to predict future aerospace employment statistics on the basis of recent world events.

- An entrepreneur develops a revolutionary new product, with no applicable demand history, and decides how many units to manufacture on the basis of an intuitive hunch.

- An astrologer advises a client to be cheerful but cautious during the next three months, a course of action that seems to be favored by the configuration of the heavens at the time of the client's birth.

It is clear that these examples are based on very different assumptions, but they have one feature in common: They represent attempts to predict some aspect of the future, based on what the forecaster believes to be the best data available. As you will learn in the following chapters, the examples represent several distinct methods of forecasting. Some methods might sound more rational and scientific than others, but no one method works best (or worst) under all circumstances.

Some authors draw a distinction between use of the terms *forecasting* and *prediction*, whereas others limit the term *forecasting* to mean projections based on past data. Still another school of thought maintains that the future cannot be predicted at all because it is determined by our present actions.[1] These definitions are too philosophical for our purposes. In this book, the term *forecasting* refers to any attempt to predict or estimate some future event, using any method that comes to hand. But we will focus mainly on the forecasting methods that businesses have found practical.

WHY FORECAST?

Prophets, oracles, soothsayers, and individuals with similar titles have been said to constitute the world's second oldest profession. It's hardly necessary to explain why people want to know what will happen in the future.

There are obvious financial advantages in being able to predict trends in the stock market, interest rates, or real estate. Everyone tries to forecast, but only the successful ones get rich. Similarly, the ability to forecast product demand can save you a lot of money through proper inventory control. If you fail to maintain a sufficiently high inventory level, stockouts will occur, with possible loss of future business. If you shoot for an unreasonably high service level, you can wind up with a lot of leftover stock, which will rust, become obsolete, or simply take up space.

Forecasting isn't limited to business or financial situations, however. Law enforcement agencies would like to be able to predict when terrorist groups are most likely to strike, where the next in a series of consumer fraud operations will arise, or what conditions tend to favor recidivism. On a more personal level, it would be desirable to be able to predict the most favorable time to travel by air or to change jobs. Some of these forecasting goals are more feasible than others, but each has been the subject of diligent effort.

DOES FORECASTING WORK?

Throughout history, every tribe has included a few individuals who questioned the pronouncements of the soothsayer. Careful examination of his[2] forecasts revealed that many of them were wrong, unless he was shrewd enough to surround them with a hedge of Delphic generalities in the first place. Nor was everyone taken in by his personal charisma, or by his attempts at Monday morning quarterbacking. Many felt that it was his job to know in advance that the spirits would be angry.

Similarly, forecasters appear to have a slightly unsavory image in some present-day organizations. At least one author has gone so far as to state that "Forecasts are always wrong."[3] Modern forecasters may speak of large error terms and faulty sampling methodology, rather than of angry spirits, but the bottom line is often the same: the forecast didn't work.

The introduction of mathematical models and digital computers has given forecasting a mystique that it scarcely deserves, for human judgment remains the most crucial element in any forecast. Computers perform calculations far faster and more accurately than any human being, and they are essential tools in modern forecasting, but the forecaster still must decide what data and assumptions will go into the model. Indeed, the best forecasting software package on the market will yield terrible results if the user does not understand what he or she is doing.

Recent studies tend to confirm what managers have always suspected: the most important factor affecting forecast accuracy is not the method, but the person. For short-term sales forecasting, people with more formal training in forecasting tend to get better results.[4] In other forecasting situations, however, the factors responsible for success are less obvious.

THE MAN IN THE FEATHERED HAT

The senior author will now speak.

> Some twenty years ago, on a bus in Berkeley, California, I met a prosperous man who wore a curious feathered hat. I never learned why he wore feathers, or why he rode the bus; but he carried a thick wad of hundred-dollar bills such as I had never seen before. He had won these at the racetrack, and he attributed his success to the use of a slide rule.
>
> I was impressed, because the gentleman showed little evidence of formal schooling; whereas I, a university student recently graduated from one of San Francisco's finest finishing schools, had not mastered the use of this device. In the manner of a fellow professional, I asked him to share his forecasting technique with me.
>
> It turned out that he used the slide rule in the same way that a dowser uses a forked stick to find water. He waved it around his head three times, muttering something that sounded remarkably like a voodoo curse, and then allowed it to point to the name of the winning horse.
>
> I reflected on the fact that, regardless of the mathematical validity of this technique, the slide rule was in fact selecting the right horses more often than chance alone would predict. Probably the divining rod principle was in effect: Consciously or not, the man was directing the instrument, and his own considerable knowledge of the horses was responsible for his success. The slide rule merely increased his confidence, by projecting his own thoughts into the spirit world of mathematics. But in the hands of someone who lacked this knowledge, the same technique would have failed.

Forecasting can work fairly well; it often does. To make it work, however, the business forecaster must understand the factors that influence the data with which he or she is working. Given this background, the forecaster can recognize whether or not a mathematical forecasting procedure is working properly, by looking at the output, and can override the results if necessary. (If the slide rule started to point to the wrong horse, the man in the feathered hat would redirect it.)

Ignoring a faulty model is far better than allowing it to run amok—but ignoring it is not nearly as good as understanding it and fixing it. An understanding of the *data* is the first requirement of a good forecaster. The second requirement, the focus of this book, is an understanding of the *tools* that are available for analyzing those data.

Many business forecasters, like the man in the feathered hat, understand the data but not the tools. A company may pay a great deal for sophisticated forecasting software that winds up being used as decoration because no one understands or trusts it. The forecaster flourishes a few graphs and printouts, and then goes ahead and uses his or her own judgment.

Unaided human judgment is good, but often it is not good enough in a highly competitive market.

WHO FORECASTS?

Ideally, the forecaster should have extensive formal training in statistics and perhaps also in computer science. In addition, he or she should have a thorough understanding of the specific business application for which the forecast is intended—for example, knowledge of a product line, its demand history, and the various factors that are likely to influence its sales.

In practice, however, few individuals know all these things. Typically the forecaster is either an academic statistician with little knowledge of business or a business manager with little knowledge of statistics. Some organizations ask their computer programmers to generate forecasts, using either a commercial forecasting software package or a textbook formula translated uncritically into a language such as BASIC. However, the programmer might be unfamiliar with both statistics and business. Still other companies forgo mathematics altogether and ask their salesmen or executives to make forecasts, using one or more of the judgmental techniques discussed in chapter 5.

In many organizations, forecasting is a team effort. When the statistician and the market specialist are two (or more) different people, effective communication between them is crucial. A survey conducted in the mid-1970s revealed that forecasters tended to rate their own performance much more highly than did the decision makers who used the forecasts[5]. The forecasters believed that they understood the decision makers' problems and requirements, but the decision makers felt otherwise. Conversely, the decision makers felt that they understood forecasting methodology fairly well, but the forecasters disagreed. (Despite these discrepancies, however, there was general agreement that communication between the two groups was adequate.)

CONSULTANTS

Equilibrists lie here; stranger, tread light.

— John Crowe Ransom

Relatively few managers have extensive training in statistics or are interested in acquiring such training. At the same time, most smaller businesses cannot afford or justify a full-time statistician. Thus forecasting is one area in which many companies can make excellent use of temporary consultants.

The forecasting consultant should have a thorough knowledge of statistics and should also be familiar with business forecasting applications. He or she should be aware of the limitations of the real world; the client is unlikely to be able to provide the consultant with twenty years' worth of impeccable data, for example, nor will all decision makers appreciate having to deal with interval forecasts, despite their theoretical merits.

The consultant should be able to explain mathematical concepts in everyday terms—or, like any successful prophet, he or she should inspire such trust and confidence that no explanation is required.

The client also has responsibilities, chief among which is the need to communicate exactly what it is that the consultant is expected to do. (We have often had clients approach us with requests such as "Here, do some statistics on this and make it look good.")

In order to know what he or she wants the consultant to do—and to be able to verify that the consultant is doing it—the manager should learn the names of some of the forecasting procedures that are available and what each of them does.

SUMMARY

Forecasting is defined as any attempt to predict future events. If an organization assigns its forecasting function to one individual, he or she should understand statistics, computers, and business. If the forecaster is a committee, it should include representatives from all these fields. Most forecasters do not need to perform calculations, because inexpensive computer programs are available to handle that aspect of the job. The forecaster's judgment is crucial in deciding which method to use.

REVIEW QUESTIONS

1. What is forecasting?

2. Who is responsible for forecasting in your organization?

3. Are computers likely to make the forecaster's job obsolete? Explain your answer.

4. As a general rule, would you prefer a forecast that was based on a mathematical model, or one that was made by a group of people using their best judgment? Explain your answer.

ENDNOTES

1. S. C. Wheelwright and S. Makridakis, *Forecasting Methods for Management* (New York: John Wiley & Sons, 1985).

2. The masculine pronoun will be used on occasion to represent an individual of unspecified gender.

3. G. W. Plossl, "Getting the Most From Forecasts," paper presented at the International Conference of the American Production and Inventory Control Society, 1972.

4. H. R. White, *Sales Forecasting: Timesaving and Profit-Making Strategies That Work* (Glenview, Illinois: Scott, Foresman and Company, 1984), 10

5. S. C. Wheelwright and D. Clarke, "Corporate Forecasting: Promise and Reality," *Harvard Business Review*, November-December 1976: 40 ff.

2
Historical
Background

Witchcraft always has a hard time, until it becomes established and changes its name.

— Charles Fort

This chapter will introduce you to the following topics:

- How forecasting originated.

- How it has evolved over the years.

- How it has sometimes failed to do so.

ROOTS

The science of forecasting has a very long history. In the broadest possible sense, it may be several million years old. In the mathematical sense, it is at least 20,000 years old. Our research has uncovered the following items of interest:

- A notched reindeer antler, found in a Paleolithic cave in France, might represent one of mankind's earliest attempts at time series forecasting. Scientists think that early man possibly counted days in order to be able to predict certain events, such as the arrival of game herds.

- The American Statistical Association, founded in 1839, is one of the oldest professional organizations in America. It has a fascinating emblem with a couple of snakes on it. (In this context, snakes are supposed to represent wisdom rather than evil.)

- The ancient Romans used animal intestines for forecasting. Guts are still a prerequisite of the job.

HISTORY

Western mathematicians have studied time series since the beginning of the nineteenth century. One of the first practical applications of this new science was the analysis of sunspot cycles.[1] The procedure used at that time was akin to harmonic analysis, a forerunner of modern spectral analysis (chapter 6). By about 1900, these principles were being applied to a variety of natural cyclic phenomena.

In the 1930s, mathematicians developed the autoregressive-moving average models which were popularized some forty years later by Box and Jenkins, and which have confounded business managers ever since. The first spectral analysis and adaptive filtering models were proposed in the 1940s. Exponential smoothing was developed in the late 1950s.

In its early days, time series analysis found support in some unusual circles. The occult fringe—which has always been fond of things like the Number of the Beast—seized happily on the notion that numbers not only reflected events in the real world, but actually *caused* those events. This idea can be traced all the way back to the ancient Egyptians and Greeks, who believed that mathematical relationships had religious as well as practical significance.[2]

In the last years of World War II, the U.S. military started putting mathematicians in charge of some fairly awesome projects. If a statistical process like neutron emission could ruin your whole day, maybe numbers had divine powers after all. This idea, which had never really died out, experienced a pale resurgence.

In his famous short story *The Year of the Jackpot*, science fiction writer Robert Heinlein cast his hero as a statistical consultant—perhaps one of the few times that our profession has been so honored. In the story, the statistician decided to draw graphs of all the world's cyclic phenomena, such as sunspots, snowshoe hare populations, weather, and incidents of eccentric human behavior. Then he noticed that a day was approaching when all the peaks and valleys of all the various graphs would coincide. The result? The world was destroyed.

There is something about the mystique of numbers, and the wonderfulness of graphs, and the whole idea of cause and effect, that makes perfectly nice people go berserk. When you get to the chapter on causal models, please be careful.

MANKIND DISCOVERS TOOLS

Most of us nowadays take calculators for granted, even if we are not on friendly terms with computers. It's hard to imagine how the earliest forecasters managed without so much as an efficient adding machine. Even within recent memory, life was not easy for the statistician.

In 1973, one of the authors of this book discovered a new species of chipmunk. This author will now speak.

> Actually the chipmunks had been there all along, running around the woods for millennia. All I did was to notice some variations that no one else had seen before. Instead of one kind of animal, there were two; and as I went higher up the mountain, their tails became shorter. If you are good at noticing things like this, you have the soul of a forecaster. (You can also expect an uneven sort of life.)
>
> So I measured a lot of tails that year, and when I was finished, I wanted to analyze my data using something called a discriminant function. A major American museum granted me $450.00 for data processing costs and advised me not to spend it all in one place.
>
> So I invested $40.00 in my first calculator—which could not do any of the fancy things that calculators do nowadays—and allocated the rest of the money to living expenses for the next six months. Then I sat down with a large stack of paper and a book on matrix algebra. Three days later, I understood why so many people hate statistics. I knew God didn't make me for this.

THE GOOD OLD DAYS

The greatest task before civilization at present is to make machines what they ought to be, the slaves, instead of the masters of men.

—Havelock Ellis

Younger readers may not be aware that programmable calculators and microcomputers were hard to come by in 1973. All that a reasonably priced calculator could do was add, subtract, multiply, and divide. When independent statisticians of that era needed access to a computer, we had to apply for an account on the mainframe system at a university computer center. The cost usually was high, unless a sponsor picked up the tab.

Next, we would try to locate some documentation on the resident statistical software package. This documentation invariably was shredded and partly missing, and the pages that remained would baffle a Rhodes scholar.

Then we would spend several days punching our data and job control language statements onto a stack of Hollerith cards. Much of this time was spent waiting for an available keypunch machine. An old-fashioned keypunch was a hostile thing to use, too, because the only way to correct errors was to start over with a new card.

We would give the finished stack of cards to a gnome who emerged every so often from a very cold room that users were not allowed to enter. As the door opened, we were treated to tantalizing glimpses of whirring machinery, flashing lights, and spinning tapes, all of them tended by similar gnomes who mumbled to themselves in a strange language.

Hours later, our stack would reappear, accompanied by a very thin printout, which stated that one of the cards had a typographic error on it and the job had been killed. Then we would retype the card and start over. We would sit around the computer lab until four o'clock in the morning, on a regular basis, eating candy bars, punching ourselves awake and running the program over and over again. Unless a mathematical procedure was very complicated or there was a great deal of data, sometimes it was faster and less frustrating to do the problem by hand.

Unfortunately, many people of our generation who do not work regularly with computers still view data processing this way. This group includes a lot of business managers and forecasters. But the world has changed. You can own a small computer and a statistical program for a few hundred dollars. It is fast and easy to use, and you have complete control over it. You can go to sleep and leave it running.

Forecasting has entered the Computer Age. Or has it?

RESISTANCE

When we became interested in business applications of statistics a few years ago, we noticed a funny thing. The forecasting methods that we had learned about in school were not being used very much in the real world.

Instead, we encountered all sorts of procedures and statistics that we had never heard of before, such as exponential smoothing and the mean absolute deviation. And when we did run across something familiar, often we found that strange formulas were being used to implement it.

When we took a closer look at some of these methods and read about how they had originated, we found that we had gone through a time warp. The methods were designed to cope with the slow computers of the early 1960s or, better yet, to circumvent the need for a computer at all. Back in those good old days, running a computer was not only slow and frustrating, it was expensive. You had to pay for CPU time, and usually you had to write your own program. Data storage media were more expensive too.

A case in point: An article written in 1987—which we won't cite, as a courtesy to the author—states that least squares regression is much more expensive to implement than exponential smoothing, because of the complexity of the mathematics and the more sophisticated computer hardware required. Baloney! You can do it on a calculator. And a book written in 1984 states that you can save lots of time and paper by using the mean absolute deviation instead of the standard deviation (see chapter 3). This is completely crazy advice.

Once you have punched in your data set, it is no more difficult to tell the computer to use one method than another. If you have access to any sort of personal computer, a $5 public domain software program will do least squares regression or find the standard deviation for you. With the amount of data you are likely to have, either of these procedures will take less than a second.

If you have thousands of data points, then, of course, it will take a bit longer. But with this much data, exponential smoothing would take a while, too. If you are a Type A personality and can't wait, then run the program at night. (Make sure the printer is turned on before you go home.)

THE HARD WAY

Here is our point. In the late 1980s, when some 90% of businesses in America have computers—depending, of course, on how you define a "business" and a "computer"—only a minority has adopted sophisticated forecasting methods that really require a computer.[3] And many others are making life unnecessarily difficult for themselves, because the shortcut methods, besides sacrificing accuracy, often are harder to understand and use than the methods they are intended to replace.

The available literature does not make it clear just how many businesses are using effective quantitative forecasting techniques. The statement that about 20% of businesses use regression, for example, is not very informative.[4] To one forecaster, the word "regression" describes any of a wide range of mathematical procedures including time series analysis. To another, it means a causal model. To still another, it means drawing a line on a piece of paper.

Also, a company may state that it owns a highly sophisticated forecasting software package, but may fail to add that no one has figured out how to use it or even feels highly motivated to try. This is a surprisingly common situation.

It is beyond the scope of this book to delve into the psychological and socioeconomic reasons for math anxiety, computer anxiety, or the general human tendency to resist change. It is within the scope of this book to describe some of the consequences of these processes, and to explain why it might be a good idea for businesses to deal with them.

COUNTER-RESISTANCE

The fact that you are reading this book suggests that you are interested in learning more about business forecasting. If the book makes sense to you, then at some point you will find yourself trying to convince someone else that some portion of it is correct. You will cite it as evidence that your company should buy some more software, or hire a statistician, or stop trying to understand Box-Jenkins, or stop relying on a forecasting method that doesn't work very well.

If you want someone to accept a new idea, do not appeal to abstract philosophy. Instead, show them what they can get out of it. Here are some of the reasons why businesses should use modern quantitative forecasting procedures:

- Contrary to the expectations of many readers, modern computer-aided forecasting methods often are *easier* to use than the older methods.

- There is a good chance that profits will increase, especially if inventory management is an important consideration in your business.

- It is good for company image and morale to use methods that are at least as up-to-date as the ones the competition uses, especially if upgrading does not require a major investment.

- In some states, at the time this book was written, you could actually apply for a cash grant to help defray the cost of training your staff to use a new computer system.

If your company already has an elaborate forecasting software package, but no one in the organization understands it or likes it, you need to find out why. At this stage you may want to hire a statistician to evaluate your system—preferably one who does not also sell software.

Computer-generated forecasts typically are ignored when they differ from the expectations of experienced people. In such a case, either the program is wrong or the people are wrong or, possibly, both are wrong:

- If the program is giving you the wrong answers, read this book and figure out why. Regression won't work on lumpy horizontal data. Box-Jenkins won't work if you have only been in business for a couple of weeks. Adaptive filtering won't work unless you understand it. Above all, ask the managers what they know that the computer doesn't. Maybe they are aware of a seasonal pattern or other factors that influence the forecast.

- If the people are wrong, then you have a problem. This is a primordial battle that you will not win. Either get a new job, or try to draw the people into the process of developing a new system. You might adopt the "final forecast" concept, in which the mathematical prediction is always tempered with human judgment before it is used as a basis for decision making.

- If both the computer and the people are wrong, insist on cash. The company has a dismal future.

SUMMARY

Forecasting is a very ancient science that has lagged behind the times. Computer technology has removed many of the obstacles that forecasters had to deal with a generation ago, but a majority of businesses have not taken advantage of this fact. Computer-aided forecasting can benefit a business in many ways, because it is often easier and more accurate than the earlier pencil-and-paper methods. Small computers and many forecasting programs are available at low cost. Even when a mathematical forecasting method is used, human judgment still must be considered.

REVIEW QUESTIONS

1. How did early computers limit the options available to forecasters?

2. Find out what forecasting methods are being used in your organization, and ask some of the users if they find these methods satisfactory.

3. How would you go about convincing an old-guard manager to try a potentially more effective forecasting method?

4. Assume that you succeed in convincing this manager to try out your method. So she spends several thousand dollars on computer hardware, software, and human resources to develop the new forecasting model. You try it out and it doesn't work any better than the old one. What should you do? (Think carefully about your answer. There may be a test later.)

ENDNOTES

1. W. Herschel,. "Observations Tending to Investigate the Nature of the Sun," *Transactions of the Royal Society of London* (1801), 265–313.

2. H. Meschkowski, *Ways of Thought of Great Mathematicians* (San Francisco: Holden-Day. 1964).

3. Telephone interview, 1988, with H. Strickholm, Manager Operations Support, IEEE, 345 East 47th Street, New York, NY 10017.

4. J. T. Mentzer, and J. E. Cox, 1984. "Familiarity, Application and Performance of Sales Forecasting Techniques," *Journal of Forecasting* 3(1984):27-36.

3
The Heart
of Democracy

Statistics are the heart of democracy.

—Simeon Strunsky (1944)

Okay, so we cheated. This chapter is really about statistics, but we felt that it needed a more interesting title.

As you read about forecasting, you will run into some statistical terms. You don't want to be caught with a foolish expression on your face when someone at a meeting starts talking about degrees of freedom or confidence intervals. This chapter is intended to make you conversant in the subject without turning you into a mathematician.

The chapter will introduce you to the following topics:

- The null hypothesis
- Degrees of freedom

—well, just read the chapter.

THE MAIN THING

If you understand just one thing about statistics, then you are ahead of the game: Statisticians talk about what is *likely* to happen, not what *will* happen. They deal in things that cannot be measured or predicted with complete accuracy. The usual reason is that there are too many of the things to measure them all, or some of them haven't happened yet.

For example, you might conduct a market survey to find out how many people like your product. You can't possibly talk to everyone in America, or to everyone in Detroit. Some people have no telephones, others are not home, and others hate surveys. Still others have not been born yet. Besides, it would cost too much money to ask everyone. This is why the national census is such a big deal.

So you look at a representative *sample* of the population that you are interested in. The population might be everybody in America, or everybody in Detroit, or just married women of Lithuanian ancestry between the ages of 26 and 28. Your sample of this population would consist of just a few of the people in it.

It is important to remember that, in statistics, a "population" might not be composed of people. You might be interested in the population of dust particles on the floor of your warehouse. Just as you could not interview everyone in Detroit, so you could not collect and measure all those little particles. But it is important that you know some accurate facts about them, because they influence the way that your machinery operates.

So you collect a sample of (say) 1,000 representative dust particles, get out a microscope, and measure their diameters. You add the measurements together and divide by 1,000. The result is the average. But the average what?

It might appear that you have learned the average size of dust on your factory floor. But you haven't. You have learned the average size of the *sample*. This is only an estimate of the true, unobservable population average. The statistician has to figure out how good the estimate is, so management can decide how much money to sink into dealing with it.

NULL HYPOTHESIS

Here is another sampling problem. You have conducted a market survey for your company, which makes rear view mirrors. You have learned that 34% of respondents in the Florida sample liked your products, but that only 22% of those in the Massachusetts sample liked them. Each sample contained 100 people.

Before you start working on a new advertising campaign, you should figure out whether the survey results really mean anything. Of course, if the survey included everyone in Florida and everyone in

Massachusetts, you wouldn't need to ask this question. The percentages would speak for themselves. But the survey didn't include everyone, just a small, representative sample from each state. You need to ask yourself what the numbers mean in terms of the whole population.

Almost anyone would put the question as follows: Are our products more acceptable to residents of Florida than to those of Massachusetts? But the statistician does not say it that way. Instead, he sets up a null hypothesis to test. In this example, the null hypothesis says: There is *no* significant difference in the level of mirror satisfaction—or whatever you wish to call it—between the two states.

"Significant" is a word that tends to annoy people. To someone in sales, it may seem obvious that a difference of twelve percentage points is important. Why test it? We are talking about millions of dollars worth of mirrors here. But again, the statistician speaks his own language. To him, *significant* doesn't mean important. A significant difference is just one that represents the whole population.

Forget mirrors for a moment. Suppose you have a hat containing ten black marbles and ten white ones. You reach in and draw four of them at random. Three are black and one is white. Does this prove that there are *significantly* more black marbles in the hat than white ones? No, it doesn't. You can't prove what is not true in the first place. Your sample just accidentally contained more black marbles.

In the same way, the statistician in our example wants to know if the mirror survey really proved anything or not. To do this, he performs a test of the null hypothesis, possibly a chi-squared test (see *Contingency Table* p. 25). Depending upon the result of the test, the statistician either accepts the null hypothesis, which means there is *no* significant difference; or he rejects the null hypothesis, which means there *is* a significant difference.

Statisticians often speak of Type I errors and Type II errors. A Type I error means rejecting the null hypothesis when it is true. A Type II error means accepting the null hypothesis when it is false.

AVERAGES

You have measured a great pile of something, such as the dust particles we mentioned earlier, and the result is a long list of numbers. Usually you think of these numbers as the individual values of a *variable*, with a one-letter name such as X or Y. So X, in this example, means "diameter of dust particles."

The first thing you probably want to know about these numbers is the average or mean. This is represented as the name of the variable with a bar over it, such as: $\overline{X}$ (read "X-bar").

You already know the most common way to find the average. You add up all the numbers and divide by how many there are. Here is an example, using just a few data values:

$$3+4+4+5+4 = 20$$
$$20 \div 5 = 4$$

This is called the *simple* average or the arithmetic mean. But there are also other kinds of averages. The median and mode are averages, sort of, but they aren't used much in forecasting. There is also the geometric average. If you are interested in these terms, you can look them up in the glossary.

Forecasters often speak of *weighted* averages. In statistics, often we need to assign different weights, or levels of importance, to different data values or variables. When you read about time series methods in chapter 6, the reasons for assigning weights will be clearer. The main thing that differentiates most forecasting methods, in fact, is the way in which the weights are determined and the rationale for doing so.

The best way to explain weighted averages is to look at a different way of calculating simple averages. If you have n numbers (in this case five), you can multiply each of them by the fraction $1/n$ and then add the results together:

$$3 \times 0.2 = 0.6$$
$$4 \times 0.2 = 0.8$$
$$4 \times 0.2 = 0.8$$
$$5 \times 0.2 = 1.0$$
$$4 \times 0.2 = 0.8$$

Weighted average = 4.0

This is the same answer we got using the regular method. In other words, for the simple average, the *weight* for each of the numbers is the same: $1/5$, or 0.2.

For the weighted average, the procedure is the same except that the weights are not all alike. Some of the measurements are assigned a higher weight, for one reason or another. But these weights still must add up to 1, just as they did for the simple average ($1/5 + 1/5 + 1/5 + 1/5 + 1/5$).

For example, if you thought the first number in the series was twice as important as the others, then you might assign it a weight of

$2/5$ (or 0.4). But then all the other weights would have to be smaller than $1/5$, to make the weights add up to 1:

$$3 \times 0.4 = 1.2$$
$$4 \times 0.15 = 0.6$$
$$4 \times 0.15 = 0.6$$
$$5 \times 0.15 = 0.75$$
$$4 \times 0.15 = 0.6$$

$$\text{Weighted average} = 3.75$$

The weighted average came out smaller than the simple average this time, because we assigned a higher weight to the value of X that happened to be the smallest value in the series, 3.

MEASURES OF DISPERSION

So you have measured a pile of things and you have calculated their average size (in one sense or another). But the average is only one of the things that you may need to know about them. Depending on what you are doing, you may also want to know whether the things are all pretty much alike, or whether they differ a lot from one another. In other words, you may want to know how much they *vary*. The usual way of doing this is to find the sample variance.

The first step is to subtract the sample mean (the average value for the sample) from each of the numbers. Then you square each of the differences, and you add up all the squared differences:

$$3-4 = -1 \qquad \text{squared:} \qquad -1 \text{ times } -1 = 1$$
$$4-4 = 0 \qquad \text{squared:} \qquad 0 \text{ times } 0 = 0$$
$$4-4 = 0 \qquad \text{squared:} \qquad 0 \text{ times } 0 = 0$$
$$5-4 = 1 \qquad \text{squared:} \qquad 1 \text{ times } 1 = 1$$
$$4-4 = 0 \qquad \text{squared:} \qquad 0 \text{ times } 0 = 0$$

$$\text{total} = 2$$

Next you divide the total by the number of data values *minus 1*, which in this case is 4. The result, $2/4 = 0.5$, is the sample variance for this list of numbers. All these steps can be summarized as a formula, if you prefer:

$$(\text{Eqn. 3-1}) \qquad \text{Sample Variance} = \Sigma \frac{(X-\overline{X})^2}{n-1}$$

The large, funny-looking "E" is really the Greek letter sigma. It just means "the sum of." The letter n means the number of data values in the sample, in this case 5.

You will need to use the *standard deviation* more often than the variance. The standard deviation is just the square root of the variance. In this case, the variance was 0.5 and the square root of 0.5 is about 0.71. You will see how the standard deviation is used when you get to the section on confidence intervals.

Some older forecasting books use something called the mean absolute deviation (MAD) instead of the standard deviation to estimate the square root of the variance. The MAD is equal to about 0.8 times the standard deviation. Put another way, the standard deviation is equal to about 1.25 times the MAD.

Studies have shown that MAD is not as good an estimator as the standard deviation. We don't know why it still appears in many forecasting books, because it has not been used by most statisticians in at least thirty years. Without using some mathematics, there is no way to explain what is wrong with the MAD, so we will just ask you to trust us.

The mean absolute percentage error (MAPE) is another method of estimating the amount of variation in a set of data. Again, you start by finding the difference between each data value and the mean value. Then you find the absolute value of each error, as for MAD. Then you divide each of these absolute errors by the mean, and multiply the result by 100 to get a percentage. Finally, you divide all of these percentages by the number of data values. MAPE is not particularly useful, but many forecasting books refer to it.

ANALYSIS OF VARIANCE (ANOVA)

> *What's past, and what's to come, is strew'd with husks*
> *And formless ruin of oblivion.*
>
> —Shakespeare, *Troilus and Cressida*

ANOVA is often used to test the significance of the results of other procedures, such as regression. Basically, ANOVA tells you how much of the variation in your data is explained by the model that you are using. (Your goal is to find a model that explains as much of the variation as possible.)

Many statistical software packages automatically print what is called an ANOVA table along with the results of a regression analysis. Usually, you can ignore most of the values in the ANOVA table and just look at the F value and the p value. These will be labeled on the printout.

The F value is the ratio between two numbers. The first one, which goes on the top of the ratio, represents the amount of variation that is explained by the model. The second number, the one that goes on the bottom, represents the amount of variation that isn't explained by the model. Thus a high F value generally means that the model is doing a good job, and a low F value means the model has fallen short.

But how high must the F value be? This is where the p value comes in. It tells you the *probability* that an F value as high as the one in question could have resulted from chance alone. You want p to be low, just as you want F to be high.

The p value is taken from a table of F values which can be found in most statistics books. If you know the F value and you know how many data points there were, then you can look up the p value yourself. It is easier, however, just to let the computer do it for you. In most cases, if p is less than or equal to 0.05, then the model is considered to be okay.

CONFIDENCE INTERVALS

In statistics, often it is not good enough to state your estimate of some value (such as a forecast). It is also necessary to say how accurate that estimate is. An answer such as "real accurate" will rarely be acceptable. You need to back up your answer.

One common way to do this is to surround the estimate with a confidence interval, also called an error bound. If someone says that the value of such-and-such is 100 *plus or minus* 5, the plus or minus part is the confidence interval. There are several ways to find a confidence interval, depending on the type of problem. Here are some examples:

- You have estimated the mean annual income in Orange County, California, as $40,000. Your survey didn't include everyone in the county, so this is just an estimate. But you tried to get a representative sample—not just people driving a BMW or picking up their kids at the baby academy. Now you want to show how reliable this estimate is by surrounding it with a confidence interval.

  First, find the standard deviation of the sample data and multiply it by 2.[1] The mean *minus* two standard deviations is the lower limit of the 95% confidence interval. The mean *plus* two standard deviations is the upper limit of the 95% confidence interval.

  If the standard deviation is 7,000, the interval is 40,000 ± 14,000, or the range 26,000 to 54,000. So you can state with 95% confidence that the true average annual income for Orange County lies somewhere in this interval. (The confidence *level* in this case is 95%.)

- You have data regarding Navy missile firings, showing the numbers of successes and failures. The Navy wants to know the proportion of successful firings, with a 95% confidence interval. This is a different kind of problem, but you find the confidence interval the same way, except that the computer uses a different formula for the standard deviation. The 95% confidence interval is the percentage of successful firings, plus or minus two standard deviations.

- You are using regression to predict the number of umbrellas sold per day on the basis of rainfall the previous day. Just showing your boss the answer that you get is not good enough. You must also tell her how accurate the forecast is. It may be less obvious in this case how you find the confidence interval, so we will explain.

Suppose that you have data for rainfall and umbrella sales every day for the past year, and you need to predict sales for tomorrow. So you call the Weather Service and ask how many inches of rain fell in your city today. Then you plug the number of inches of rain into your regression equation—which will be defined later in the chapter—and out pops the number of umbrellas which you expect to sell tomorrow.

Now you have a forecast—but this forecast actually represents the *average* number of umbrellas that you would expect to sell, given lots of different days with this amount of rainfall. How good is the estimate?

An estimate of a mean, like an estimate of anything else, has a standard deviation. This is all you need to make a confidence interval. But the formula for this kind of standard deviation is unusually long and horrible, so you won't find it in this book. Just ask your friendly statistical program to do it for you.

Returning to the previous example, which involved umbrella sales: Suppose that there was one-half inch of rain today and your model predicts that the store will sell 230 umbrellas tomorrow, with a standard deviation of 33 umbrellas. The 95% confidence interval is 230 ± 66, or 164 to 296 umbrellas.

What this means is the following: On 95% of all business days that follow a day with one-half inch of rain, you can expect to sell somewhere between 164 and 296 umbrellas. Your level of confidence in this estimate, then, is 95%. The *upper limit of confidence* is 296. This is the number of umbrellas you need to have in stock if you want to be 95% certain of not running out.

But suppose that you need a higher level of confidence than this. Your boss might want to be almost totally certain that she will not run out of umbrellas. She doesn't mind wasting money or space on possible extra umbrellas. Then you might want to use the 99% confidence level instead. For this level, you need 2.6 standard deviations on either side of your estimate. (You might think of this as casting a wider net to be sure of catching more possible outcomes.)

The number 230 plus or minus 2.6 standard deviations, in this case, defines the interval 144 to 316. Therefore, to be 99% confident of not running out, you should have 316 umbrellas on the shelf. But, you might sell only 144 of them and have an awful lot of umbrellas left over.

This is why businesses so often run out of some item. In order to be *absolutely* sure of not running out, they would have to set the confidence level extremely high. This could mean a great deal of money tied up in inventory and, depending on the product, a lot of expense connected with storing the items or disposing of moldy leftover ones.

DEGREES OF FREEDOM

When you get right down to it, this is a somewhat difficult concept. It is possible to use the term correctly, however, without having the remotest idea of what it means. You can think of the degrees of freedom as a number in a table, period.

When you do a statistical test, using a calculator or a pencil and paper, typically you need to look up a value in a table in a book. To read the table correctly, you need to know the number of degrees of freedom of the data.

But if you know how to do the test in the first place, you have been reading a statistics book; and the book also tells you how to find the number of degrees of freedom for that particular test. Or if you have followed our advice and bought some forecasting software, then you will not need to calculate the degrees of freedom or look in the table anyway. The printout will tell you how many degrees of freedom there were, often using the abbreviation *d.f.*

We will explain the term for those who are interested. If you are an engineer, you know that *degrees of freedom* is a term also used in mechanics. There, it refers to the number of independent ways a mechanical system can move without violating any rules or constraints. In statistics, it means sort of the same thing. In the mirror example earlier in the chapter, there were four classes of people:

Florida—liked

Florida—didn't like
Massachusetts—liked
Massachusetts—didn't like

A total of 200 opinions was recorded. This can't change, or "move." Therefore, only three of the four classes can change freely. When these change, the fourth one has to change by a set amount—the amount required for the total to remain 200. So there are three degrees of freedom in this problem.

CONTINGENCY TABLE

This is a way of arranging certain kinds of data so that you can perform a chi-square test on them. A chi-square test is used to compare some groups of things, to find out whether or not some event occurs more often in one group than in another. We mentioned this in the rear view mirror example. (The test gets its name from the Greek letter chi or χ, which is used in the calculations.)

For example, you might have data on ten of your company's 1984 trucks and ten of its 1985 trucks, all of which were involved in head-on collisions. If five of the 1984 trucks exploded on impact, but only three of the 1985 ones did, are the 1985 trucks really better? Or was the difference just random?

To answer the question, you could set up a contingency table and apply the chi-square test. The table might look like this:

	1984	1985	Totals
Exploded	5	3	8
Didn't	5	7	12
Totals	10	10	20

It would make no difference if you stood the table on its edge, so that the years were down the side like this:

	Exploded	Didn't	Totals
1984	5	5	10
1985	3	7	10
Totals	8	12	20

In either case, this is called a 2 × 2 contingency table, because there are two numbers across and two down. There are two rows (R) and two columns (C) of data in the table, not including the totals. Each of the little boxes in the table, containing one data value, is called a *cell*. This table has four cells. (The totals are not considered to be inside cells.)

The table alone looks okay for our purposes. It seems to show that 50% ($5/10$) of the 1984 trucks blew up on impact, but only 30% ($3/10$) of the 1985 trucks did. Not great, but we will work on it.

Next, you can test the data by plugging them into the chi-square formula. (This formula is very simple, but it is even simpler to let your statistical program do it for you, so we'll skip it.)

In this example, the computer printout or screen display would show that the chi-square value is about 0.834 and that the corresponding p value is greater than 0.25. We talked about p values before. In this case, the p value means that there is more than a 25% chance that the two groups of trucks represent pretty much the same population after all. Remember, these two groups of trucks are just *samples* of all the trucks that were involved (or could have been) in head-on collisions during those two years.

The null hypothesis says there is no significant difference between trucks for the two years. You hoped to be able to reject this hypothesis, because you would like to think that the trucks had improved. But because the p value is much greater than 0.05—in fact, it's greater than 0.25—you cannot reject the hypothesis. In ordinary terms, then, there isn't any real difference between the proportion of trucks that exploded in 1984 and those that exploded in 1985. The difference is just random variation.

Since there isn't a lot of data in this table, the results may not mean much, one way or the other. But we will proceed anyway, because your employer needs to respond to a consumer protection agency that thinks the trucks may not be safe. And you cannot present the results as they stand; they would look terrible. So you decide to edit the data just a little. (This is a procedure that we do *not* encourage in real life. But just as it takes a thief to catch one, a good forecaster must know how to cheat.)

You ask a few questions and find that, in two of the 1985 truck accidents, there was a remote possibility that the driver was carrying an explosive chemical. Probably those two trucks would have blown up anyway. So you remove them from the cell containing 1985 trucks that exploded.

Now that you have removed these two data points from the "exploded" cell, you might expect to throw them out altogether. But you can improve the appearance of the table even more by giving the two trucks the benefit of the doubt, and implying that they did not really explode at all. Then you can move them to the "didn't" cell. (If asked about this, you can explain that the explosions were irrelevant to the analysis because they did not reflect problems in engineering design, or something like that.) Here is the revised table:

	Exploded	Didn't	Totals
1984	5	5	10
1985	1	9	10
Totals	6	14	20

You can see that this table has great potential even before we get to the chi-square test. Clearly, 50% of the 1984 trucks exploded but only 10% of the 1985 trucks did. Or put another way, the 1985 trucks are five times as good!

Repeating the calculations will show that the chi-square value is now about 3.81. In the chi-square table, the critical value for our purposes turns out to be 3.84. Well, this is close enough. Just round it off, and you can reject the null hypothesis. Your employer will triumphantly claim that an independent statistician has verified the results.

Incidentally, the test we have just performed is not valid. The reason is that there are not enough data values. We neglected to mention that, as a rule of thumb, you need at least five values in each cell of a contingency table for the results to mean anything. One cell in our table contained only a single value.

But if someone still questions your conclusion, insisting that the improvement in the 1985 trucks was not significant, then you can produce your trump card. You can reply that it was significant *to the people who died*. This will effectively sidestep the mathematical issue.

PATTERNS OF DISTRIBUTION

A list of numbers has an average and a certain amount of variation. It also has a certain shape, or distribution, if you plot all the numbers on a graph. In other words, some values occur more often than others. There are lots of different kinds of distributions.

If your company sells shoes, for example, you need to predict more than just the number of shoes that people will buy next year. You might also need to know how many people have big feet, average feet, and so on, so that you can order the right distribution of sizes.

If you expected to sell the same number of each size shoe, you would call this a uniform distribution. Then you would stock an equal number of each size. Or if everyone wore size 8, this would be a monotonic distribution. You would order just size 8. Intuition probably tells you, however, that neither is the right answer. Instead, there are a few "medium" sizes that account for a disproportionate number of sales. There is a lower level of demand for shoes that are smaller or larger. This trend is more pronounced for sizes that are extremely small or extremely large.

Measurements of products like shoes, clothes, horse collars, and tomatoes tend to follow what is called a *normal distribution*. The reason is that most living things are medium. The norm means the average, or something near the average. You can see why the word "normal" also has acquired an ethical connotation.

Aside from any philosophical problems, the normal distribution is helpful to the forecaster. Whatever the product, if the distribution is normal, the data values form a predictable bell-shaped graph.

Living things and their paraphernalia provide some of the easiest examples of the normal distribution. It turns out, however, that (for reasons we won't go into) many other kinds of products are also distributed this way. For example, if your company makes silicon wafers, the numbers of defective integrated circuits on each wafer form a bell-shaped curve. The yield for most of the wafers falls in a certain range in the middle of the graph. Then there are a few wafers with a lot more bad circuits than this, or a lot less.

In more general terms, Fig. 3-1 is a graph of the numbers of defective widgets in 100 lots of widgets. The bars in the graph approximate a sort of lumpy bell. The same shape graph could represent lots of other things.

If you aren't familiar with bell-shaped curves, think about this one for a moment. The high central part of the "bell" represents the large group of medium values. The low outer edges of the bell are the relatively rare items—in this case, the lots that contain more bad widgets than expected, or fewer.

Some statistical tests and procedures work only if the data are normally distributed, so this is something you may need to consider at some point. When we talked about confidence intervals, for example, we were assuming a normal distribution.

You can get a rough idea about the distribution just by drawing a graph, with the values along the horizontal axis and the frequency up the side. If the result is more or less bell- shaped, probably the data follow a normal distribution. But a true normal distribution has other characteristics besides being shaped like a bell, so you may need to test further by running a statistical program designed for this purpose.

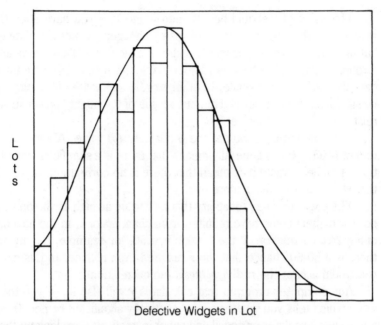

L
o
t
s

Defective Widgets in Lot

Fig. 3-1. Sample Data Showing Normal Distribution Curve.

The normal distribution is not the only one you may encounter in forecasting. Certain kinds of related problems involve the binomial, Poisson, Weibull, and other distributions. These are discussed briefly in the Glossary.

CORRELATION AND REGRESSION

These are two terms that the forecaster must understand. People are always getting the two concepts mixed up, but they are not the same thing at all.

If two variables X and Y are *correlated*, this simply means that they are associated in some way, so that if one changes, the other also changes. The strength of this association is reflected in a number called the correlation coefficient, or r.

Calculating the correlation coefficient r is simple, but somewhat tedious—the kind of task for which computers were designed. Almost all statistical programs do it. Many programmable calculators also come with a standard routine for calculating r. The reader who insists on doing it by hand may use the following formula:

$$\text{(Eqn. 3-2)} \quad r = \frac{\Sigma \, (X-\overline{X}) \, (Y-\overline{Y})}{\sqrt{\Sigma \, (X-\overline{X})^2 \, (Y-\overline{Y})^2}}$$

The value of r should be between 0 and 1, if you have done the math correctly. The hard part, for many managers, is not calculating r but figuring out what it means. A higher r value doesn't always mean a stronger relationship between two variables, because the amount of data also makes a difference. In other words, an r value of 0.9 may not be significant for one set of data, but a value of 0.4 might show a strong relationship for another set.

The solution is to look at the probability (p) value. A low p value (below 0.05 or 0.01) generally means that there is a significant correlation. A higher p value may mean that there is no correlation, or simply that you need to look at more data.

The p value is the probability that an r value as high as the one you got (or higher) could have resulted from chance alone, in the absence of any real correlation. If the p value is 0.50, for example, this means there is a 50-50 chance that the r resulted from chance. In this case, you would accept the *null hypothesis* (no correlation).

Any computer program that calculates r will also show you the p value which tells you whether r is statistically significant or not. If you are using a calculator or pencil and paper instead, you can look up the r value in a table in a statistics book or in any book of standard mathematical tables, such as the *CRC Manual*.

If you find the square of r, you will then have a parameter known as r^2, R^2, or the *coefficient of determination*. This is a very useful statistic to pull out of your hat during a business meeting, because it has a clear intuitive meaning for many people. It is said to represent the percentage of variation in the data which is explained by the model.

If r is 0.8, for example, then r squared is 0.64, which means that 64% of the variation in the data is explained by the model that you have proposed. You can make a statement like this to show how good your model is, or how bad somebody else's model is.

Unfortunately, R^2 is often abused and misinterpreted. One author describes the coefficient of determination as ''an inflated measure of the goodness of fit'' and reviews several alternative methods of calculating it to avoid this problem[2].

Regression, on the other hand, describes *how* the variables are associated, not just how strongly they are associated. Does Y increase when X increases, or does it decrease? And by how much? And what shape is the graph—straight or curved?

We will talk about regression mainly in chapters 6 and 7, because it is often used as a forecasting method. Right now, we will focus on how it works. With this background, you will have a better idea of how to use it later on.

If there are just two variables, then this is called simple regression, and the relationship can be represented as a straight or curved line. The values of the independent variable, called X, are graphed along the horizontal axis. In forecasting, often the X variable is time. The other variable is called Y, and it is graphed along the vertical axis. It is called the dependent variable.

Unlike correlation, regression cannot be described by a single number. It can be described with a picture or, better yet, with an equation. In either case, you need to know two things: the slope or angle of the line, and where it is located on the graph paper. You may also want to know how much of the variation in Y is not explained by changes in X. If not much of it is explained, then the regression model isn't doing you much good.

For simple regression, the general equation looks like this:

$$\text{(Eqn. 3-3)} \qquad Y = a + bX + e$$

In this equation, a is the point where the line would cross the Y axis. In other words, it is the value of Y when X is zero. The symbol b represents the slope of the line, and e is the error term (the unexplained variation). In a real regression model, there would be numbers in place of a and b.

In many books, a is called the Y intercept and b is called the regression coefficient. Often they are represented by other letters, too, but this makes no difference.

Looking at Equation 3-3 for a few minutes can tell you something about regression. For example, suppose the line doesn't "slope" at all. It's a flat line across the page, with no trend. The flat line here means about the same thing that it does to an emergency medical technician: your hypothesis is dead. The slope b is equal to zero and Y remains equal to a. This makes sense, because a was the value of Y at the beginning of the time period that you are looking at. There was no trend, so it stayed there.

Least squares regression is the best-known method for calculating the values of a and b. We hope that you will let your computer do these calculations, because they are tedious, but here are the formulas if you want them:

$$\text{(Eqn. 3-4)} \quad \text{Slope} = b = \frac{\Sigma (X - \overline{X})\,(Y - \overline{Y})}{\Sigma (X - \overline{X})^2}$$

$$\text{(Eqn. 3-5)} \quad Y \text{ intercept} = a = \overline{Y} - b\overline{X}$$

You use analysis of variance, as explained in a previous section, to find out whether the resulting values are significant or not. We are not going to work through a numerical example of this. Again, you can let your program do it or look it up in a statistics book.

Because regression defines the relationship between two or more variables—say, time and sales—it is often used in forecasting. That is, if you know how sales figures are likely to change over time, you can predict sales at some specified time in the future. This use of regression is often called trend line analysis.

Suppose that you have twelve months of sales data and you want to determine if sales are increasing over time. Sales of brass widgets for January through December are as follows:

75, 100, 90, 110, 110, 125, 140, 130, 130, 125, 110, 150

You start by plotting all the points, as shown in Fig. 3-2. The result is called a scatter plot. (Most people like to graph their data before doing anything else with it.)

In order to calculate r, you need to convert the months to numbers, because a word such as "June" cannot be used in mathematical operations. The months should be assigned the numbers 1 through 12, as shown on the graph.

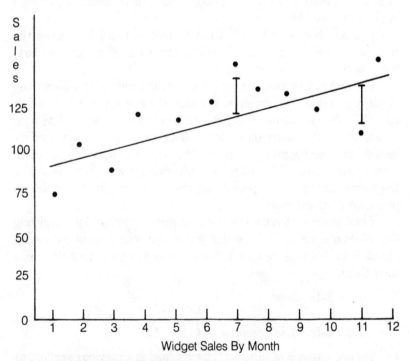

Widget Sales By Month

Fig. 3-2. Scatter Plot With Regression Line.

Usually you will want to look at the value of *r* as well as the regression equation. When your computer or calculator plugs these particular data values into the formula for *r*, it will get the value 0.79.

Taken at face value, this appears to be a fairly high correlation coefficient. The significance of the number, however, depends on how much data went into it. If we had only two or three data values, few people would intuitively trust the result. If we had thousands of values, then the trend would clearly be a strong one. But what about twelve? Is this enough, or not?

The solution is to check the *p* value, which is the probability that the twelve values just happened to arrange themselves this way by accident. The *p* value usually appears on the screen along with the correlation coefficient and other information. In this case it is only 0.002, so we reject the null hypothesis. In other words, the correlation is significant.

Similarly, the computer will come up with something like the following regression equation:

$$Y = 85.91 + 4.67X$$

This equation describes the line that we have drawn through the middle of our scatter plot in Fig. 3-2. (The error term *e* hasn't really gone away, but you don't need it to calculate *Y*.) You can check this by plugging in the *X* values, 1 through 12, and convincing yourself that the resulting points fall on the line.

Why is the method called least squares? The idea is to find the line that fits the data as closely as possible. When we say that a line *fits* the data, we mean that the sum of the squared deviations is smaller than it would be for any other line. Now let us examine this statement to see exactly what it means:

A *deviation* is just the distance between an actual data point and the nearest point on the regression line that goes past it. We have indicated two of these distances in Fig. 3-2. Now if you take a deviation and square it, obviously you have a squared deviation. If a data point is 5 units away from the line (above or below it), then that deviation squared is equal to 25. The direction of the deviation doesn't matter, because −5 squared would be the same as +5 squared.

There is one deviation for each data point. There are twelve data points in this graph, so there would be twelve deviations if we had drawn them all. When you square each of these and add all the results together, then you have a sum of squares. This is an expression that is kicked around a great deal in statistics, so it is best to become comfortable with it early on. We used it for calculating the variance, for example.

Now the origin of the expression *least squares analysis* becomes clear: It is a method for finding the line that has the smallest possible sum of squares—the least sum of squares, or least squares for short. It turns out that Equations 3-3 and 3-4 produce the line with the smallest sum of squares. Again, we aren't going to explain why. If you have a computer, you won't ever need to refer to these formulas.

SQUARES

Students often ask why statisticians are so fond of finding the squares of numbers. There are many reasons, but two of them should be apparent from the graph:

First, any number greater than 1 becomes larger when you square it, but a large number, when squared, becomes *very* large. For example, a deviation of 4 may not seem much greater than a deviation of 1, but its square is sixteen times as large. Therefore, by squaring the deviations, we assign more importance to the big ones than to the small ones.

Second, by squaring the values, we make them all positive. Otherwise, the negative deviations would tend to cancel out the positive ones and the sum would be zero, which would not be very useful for most purposes.

TIME SERIES

If you measure some Y variable at equally spaced points in time, the model is called a time series model. Sometimes it is represented in the form of Equation 3-2, with the independent variable X equal to time periods 1, 2, 3, etc. In other cases, however, a time series model is written like this:

$$(\text{Eqn. 3-6}) \quad Y_t = b_1 Y_{(t-1)} + b_2 Y_{(t-2)} + \ldots + b_n Y_{(t-n)}$$

This may seem hopeless, but it is really very simple if you take a relaxed look at it.

At first glance, it seems that the X and the a have both vanished, so you might wonder how it can possibly represent the same sort of model as Equation 3-3. The difference has to do with some assumptions that you make about the data.

The letter t stands for time, just as X did in our example of trend line analysis. So Y_t means "the value of Y at time t." When you are reading it out loud, you say "Y sub t." The values of t are in the range 1 through n, where n is the number of equally spaced data values that you have. The dots mean that we didn't feel like writing out all the terms on the right-hand side of the equation. The computer uses them all, however, when it solves the problem.

In other words, the model tells you the relationship between the current value of Y and all of its own *past* values. It's still a regression model, but now it shows the regression of *Y* on *itself*. For this reason, it is called the autoregressive or AR model. We will have more to say about it in chapter 6.

Sometimes you tell the model to stop after a certain number of terms. The following version of the model, for example, says that Y is related to just its three most recent values:

$$Y_t = b_1 Y_{(t-1)} + b_2 Y_{(t-2)} + b_3 Y_{(t-3)}$$

The big difference between the two models is that Equation 3-6 contains lots of different b values, one for each past value of Y. In other words, it's a weighted average. In Equation 3-3, the weights are equal, even though you can't see them. The simple regression model assumes that the values of Y are independent of one another, so you can just represent them all in terms of X.

Later on, it will become more obvious what all this has to do with forecasting.

EXPONENTIAL GROWTH

You must have seen a problem like this in a Sunday supplement: If you release a single pair of mice and they reproduce every 30 days, and they have X number of baby mice per litter, how long will it take to cover the Earth to a depth of four feet in mice?

People usually think of exponential growth as something that only a scientist has to deal with. It applies to things like mice, bacteria, or the half-life of a radioactive material. But the business forecaster also may encounter exponential growth at times. Typically it occurs early in the product life cycle, before demand begins to level off.

First, let's look at growth that isn't exponential. The equation $Y = X$ is a simple equation of a straight line, because if you plug some numbers into it and then graph them, the result is a straight line. If $X = 1$, $Y = 1$. If $X = 3$, $Y = 3$, and so on. Figure 3-3a shows the graph of this equation, which is really a simple version of Equation 3-3 (with $a = 0$ and $b = 1$).

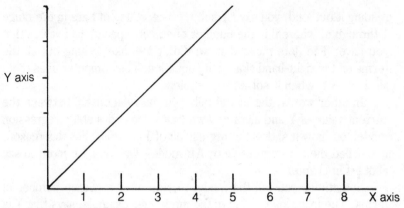

Fig. 3-3a. Graph of a Straight Line.

A graph like this is said to show linear growth. "Linear" refers to the fact that it is a straight line, and "growth" refers to the fact that Y is getting bigger as X gets bigger. (If Y were getting smaller instead, we would still call it growth, but it would be *negative* growth.)

Now if we change the equation to $Y = 2^x$, the graph will look different. It will still go up, but it will not be a straight line any more. For $X = 1$, $Y = 2$; for $X = 2$, $Y = 4$; and for $X = 3$, $Y = 8$. If we continue to plot several more points this way, the graph will look like Fig. 3-3b.

A graph that curves upward like this is said to show *exponential* growth, because the X variable is an exponent.

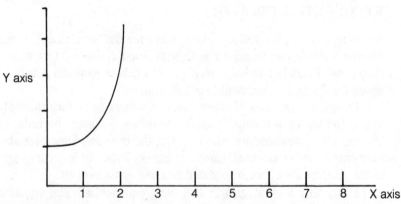

Fig. 3-3b. Exponential Growth.

GEOMETRIC GROWTH

Geometric growth often is confused with exponential growth, so the terms have come to be used interchangeably in many books. Both types of growth produce a curved graph, but they are not exactly the same.

The equation in our example of exponential growth was $Y = 2^X$. To illustrate geometric growth, we will change this to $Y = X^2$. Instead of *being* an exponent, X *has* an exponent.

The graph will look like Fig. 3-3c. This type of increase is called geometric growth, because geometry deals with squares and cubes and things like that.

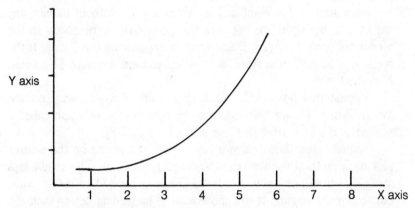

Fig. 3-3c. Geometric Growth.

GRAPHS

We have been showing you graphs for the past few pages. A graph is basically a squiggly line on paper. In cartoons, graphs always appear on the walls of executive offices and on hospital beds. (Come to think of it, in real life we have never seen a graph in either location.)

It may seem like a waste of time to explain what a graph is, but not everyone knows, and it never hurts to review a useful concept. In order to do forecasting, you must be able to draw a graph or read one that somebody else has drawn.

A *graph*, then, is simply a picture of some data, sometimes also called a plot or chart. (The three terms have slightly different connotations, which you will discover as you go along.) Graphs are widely used because many people find pictures easier to understand than columns of numbers.

The reason most graphs have two dimensions is simple: a sheet of paper is flat. A two-dimensional graph is used to show the relationship between two things, such as time and profits. These sorts of things are called variables, and one of them is designated as the X variable and the other as the Y variable.

To plot a point, such as profits for April, you would do the following. April is an expression of time, so it will almost certainly be a value of the X variable. (Whenever you graph something against time, time is plotted on the X axis by convention.) So move your pencil along the X axis until you find the point that corresponds to April. It may say April, or A, or 4 (for the fourth month of a calendar year), or something similar.

Now stop at that point and start moving up, without making any marks yet, until you are opposite the point that corresponds to the amount of profit for April. Dollar amounts appear on the Y axis. If the profit was $1 million in April, stop when you are opposite $1 million. Now draw a dot.

Repeat this process for each data point that you want on the graph. When you are finished, you will have a type of graph called a scatter graph or scatter plot (for example, Fig. 3-2).

You can stop there, or you can *smooth* the points on the scatter plot by a method such as least squares regression. The result is a straight, curved, or wavy line. If the line is generated correctly, without too much fudging, it will show what is happening better than the original scatter graph did. For example, if the data points are trending steadily upward, a nice straight line leading uphill might emphasize that fact.

Some information also will be lost at this stage, however, because the line graph will not show the individual points or the amount of variation in the data. (In many cases, concealing excessive scatter is the main point of drawing the line.)

Many readers have also seen three-dimensional graphs, which have a third axis rendered in perspective so that it appears to stick out of the page. Such graphs are used when there are three variables to consider—usually two X variables, called X_1 and X_2, which are believed to be influencing a third variable called Y. The data, in such cases, are graphed as odd-looking three-dimensional shapes. An example is shown in Fig. 3-4.

Such graphs can be very attractive and impressive, especially if they include several bright colors, so you will see a lot of them at computer trade shows and in advertisements.

Forecasting models often include more than three variables, as you will see in chapter 7. In general, however, these kinds of models can only be represented mathematically. There just isn't any reasonable way to draw a graph in four dimensions.

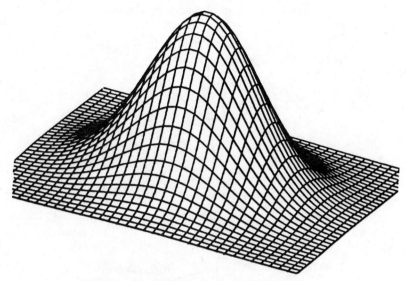

Fig. 3-4. Example of a Three-Dimensional Graph.

There are many other types of graphs. Some of them, for example, use a logarithmic scale on one or both axes. A logarithm, as you probably remember from school, is an exponent that tells the power to which a number must be raised in order to produce some other given number.

In forecasting, numbers sometimes are transformed to logarithms in order to make a graph look better or to make a mathematical procedure work. Special graph paper may be used for this purpose. *Semilog* paper has a logarithmic scale along one axis. *Log-log* paper has logarithmic scales on both axes.

The best way to find out how logarithmic transformation works is to get some graph paper of all three types, draw graphs of the same data on all three, and compare the results. Try it with data that show exponential growth and also with data that show linear growth.

Business forecasters often make use of bar graphs, line graphs, pie charts, exploded pie charts, and other graphic devices. Figure 3-1 shows an example of a bar graph, and Figs. 3-5 and 3-6 show some other useful types of graphs.

SUMMARY

Statisticians use a lot of different methods and a lot of unusual terms. The reason is that they deal in concepts that are not well represented by everyday language. The business forecaster need not be a statisti-

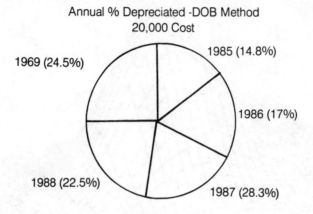

Annual % Depreciated -DOB Method
20,000 Cost

1969 (24.5%)
1985 (14.8%)
1986 (17%)
1988 (22.5%)
1987 (28.3%)

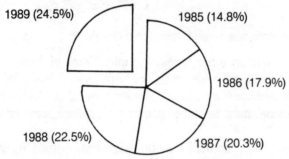

Annual % Depreciated - DOB Method
20,000 Cost

1989 (24.5%)
1985 (14.8%)
1986 (17.9%)
1988 (22.5%)
1987 (20.3%)

Fig. 3-5. Pie Charts and Exploded Pie Charts.

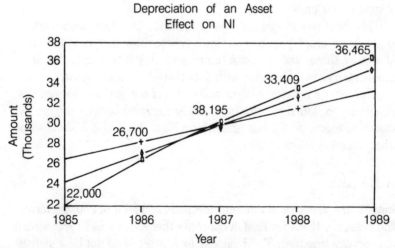

Depreciation of an Asset
Effect on NI

36,465
33,409
38,195
26,700
22,000

Fig. 3-6. Line Graph.

cian, but he or she must understand some of the major terms, just as a tourist in Mexico must speak enough Spanish to ask where the bathroom is.

REVIEW QUESTIONS

1. What is a null hypothesis? Suppose that you have been asked to develop a regression model that predicts beer sales as a function of the national unemployment rate. State your null hypothesis for this problem.

2. What does analysis of variance mean? What is it used for?

3. Why is the normal distribution referred to as a "bell-shaped curve"? Why is this distribution important to forecasters?

4. Why do you think so many formulas used by forecasters tend to use MAD rather than the standard deviation as the measure of dispersion?

5. Statisticians try to estimate values based on samples drawn from a larger population. When a forecaster looks at sales data for three years, is this a sample? If so, what is it a sample *of*? Would it be possible to look at all values in this population?

ENDNOTES

1. Actually 1.96, which is the value from the normal distribution table, but 2 is close enough.

2. J. S. Armstrong, *Long-Range Forecasting: From Crystal Ball to Computer* (New York: John Wiley & Sons, 1985), 351.

4
Deciding on a Method

There are three kinds of lies: lies, damned lies, and statistics.

— Benjamin Disraeli

This chapter will introduce you to the following topics:

- The three categories of techniques commonly used in business forecasting.

- The meanings of the terms *model* and *simulation*.

- The patterns commonly observed in time series data.

- How to choose the best forecasting method for a given situation.

DEFINITIONS

Business forecasting methods fall into three general categories: judgmental, time series, and causal.

- *Judgmental* forecasting methods are just what they sound like: methods that are based on human judgment rather than on mathematical models. Judgmental methods are sometimes also referred to as subjective or qualitative methods.

- *Time series* forecasting sometimes is called projection or extrapolation. It includes a large number of methods, all of which try to predict a future value for some variable on the basis of its *past* values only. All time series models assume that past trends will continue into the future. A simple time series model, if it works, is the easiest type of forecasting.

- *Causal* models, unlike time series models, are based on the assumption that certain events influence some other.event of interest. For our purposes, only mathematical causal models will be included in this category.

It's an axiom that all classification schemes are fuzzy. When you stop and think about it, all life is a celebration of fuzziness. And forecasting is no exception, because none of the methods we will discuss falls neatly into a single category.

Judgmental forecasting involves the interpretation of cause and effect, so it might be regarded as a causal method. Conversely, all forecasting methods involve some judgment, so they might all be considered judgmental. And there are some techniques that combine the characteristics of time series and causal models, and of course you use judgment in developing them (or deciding not to bother), so they are a combination of all three. In general, however, the three-way classification is useful.

Before we can tell you how to select a good model, we need to tell you what a model is, and what a good model is. Also, we cannot possibly define a model without telling you what a simulation is.

WHAT'S A MODEL?

It's as large as life and twice as natural.
— Lewis Carroll

The term *model*, in the mathematical sense, has become a buzz word in business. It is used so loosely that it now has virtually no meaning at all. Often it seems to refer to any method of describing, approximating, representing, or doing anything. The only prerequisite appears to be that it must contain numbers or letters or both. Ideally, it should also lend itself to presentation as a Mylar transparency.

The term cannot be avoided, however, so we must establish a definition early on. A *model*, in the restricted sense used in this book, is a mathematical representation of a relationship between two or more variables—such as time and sales. This book will describe some models in words and will present others as simplified equations. In either case they are still models, because equations are available to back them up.

There are two basic kinds of models: *stochastic* and *deterministic*. We aren't talking about forecasting models now, but about mathematical models in general. Most useful forecasting models are stochastic models, which means that they predict what is *likely* to happen under a given set of circumstances. They describe processes that involve a lot of random variation.

A deterministic model, on the other hand, describes an *exact* relationship. You must have seen a model like this:

$$P = S - M - D - A$$

where P = profits, S = sales volume, M = manufacturing costs, D = distribution costs, and A = advertising and marketing costs. In other words, if a certain amount of money comes in, and a certain amount goes out, the difference represents your profit. At least in theory, money does not simply vanish as a result of random processes.

Ohm's Law is another familiar example of a deterministic model. It defines the manner in which electrical voltage, current, and resistance are related to one another:

$$V = iR$$

If you know two of these values, you also know the third one, because it is defined by the model.

This book deals with some simple deterministic models, such as exponential smoothing, but most forecasting situations are more complicated. Here is an example:

Imagine that you want to predict how long it will take you to drive home from work today. If nothing can happen that will alter your rate of progress—if there is no traffic, if the car cannot break down, if you never speed up to read a bumper sticker, if you never have to stop for gasoline—then you can think of this as a deterministic model. Just divide the number of miles by the constant speed at which you will drive. Time equals distance divided by rate.

But you can see that this is not a useful model for forecasting purposes. It is nothing more than a formal definition of the way in which some concepts are related. Without such definitions, no one would know what anyone else was talking about. But this still doesn't tell you what time you will get home.

Common sense tells you that you cannot always predict your exact time of arrival, because a number of factors will influence your average speed. These factors might include weather conditions, your general mood, the number of cars on the road, and random things that you can't account for.

The best forecasting models are stochastic, because events in the business world are influenced by many different factors, not all of which you can predict. These random influences are often called the error term in a model.

WHAT'S A SIMULATION?

> *"If seven maids with seven mops*
> *Swept it for half a year,*
> *Do you suppose," the Walrus said,*
> *"That they could get it clear?"*
> —Lewis Carroll

The term *simulation* is another business buzz word. Like *model*, it can refer to any method of describing, approximating, representing, or doing almost anything.* Usually a simulation means a sort of trial run. First you develop a model to describe some process, and then you do a simulation to see how well your model works.

One common type of simulation, called a *Monte Carlo simulation* (chapter 5), is based on random numbers generated by the computer. Other simulations use real-life events rather than numbers on paper. Usually you substitute some event that is cheaper, safer, or easier for one that is more expensive, more dangerous, or harder to do. (If you test the exact same thing that you have modeled, then this is an experiment, not a simulation.) Several examples of simulations are described in chapter 5.

Some authors maintain that *any* forecasting method is really a simulation. The future has not happened and cannot be made to happen. In time series analysis, therefore, the model is tested with past data, which provides the best available simulation of the future. In fact, almost everything in life is a simulation. This is moderately interesting to think about.

---

*Often the two terms appear together, especially on resumes. Almost every resume we get for a computer job indicates that the person has done a lot of modeling and simulation. When we asked one applicant what kind of modeling he had done, he replied, "Platform." Another applicant had crated eggs for a living and described this as "input-output operations."

GOOD FORECASTING

From the viewpoint of most businesses, a good forecast is one that works. Chapter 8 discusses some standard techniques for keeping track of forecast accuracy and taking any necessary corrective action. But how accurate is accurate enough?

In one recent survey, more than 30% of large businesses claimed that their sales forecasts were 95 to 99% accurate over a five-year period.[1] Moreover, about 50% of *all* businesses surveyed—small, medium, and large—reported that their sales forecasts were better than 90% accurate. One large company claimed that its sales forecasts were 100% accurate.

We find these results somewhat dubious. If forecasters were this good, there would not be so many books and articles about forecasting. The sample was supposed to be representative of all American businesses, but we note that it was self-selected. That is, about 10% of all the companies that got the questionnaire decided to respond to it, and the other 90% threw it out. The ones who were doing the best job of forecasting might be more inclined to answer the questions.

Another problem is that no one can check the veracity of such statements, because forecasting records generally are kept highly confidential. People often give silly or self-aggrandizing answers to surveys, as you probably suspect if you have ever received a card from a computer dating service. (One of the authors worked for such a service many years ago. Most people who joined claimed to have exceptional—indeed, in some cases physiologically improbable—physical characteristics and an unlimited capacity for affection.) Similarly, about 80% of American workers rate their own performance as above average.[2]

We are not implying that everybody in the world is a liar. On the contrary, our own experience in taking surveys is that most people are simply polite.[3] They may have read something about the power of positive thinking. Also, they would rather give positive statements or vague euphemisms when talking to a stranger. (This is known as Mother's Rule: "If you can't say something nice, don't say anything at all.")

Another possibility is that some of the forecast survey respondents were talking about *interval forecasts*—that is, forecasts that represent a range of values rather than a single value. Interval forecasts are often a good idea, but the problem is that you can make the interval as wide as you want, and then almost any forecast can turn out to be "accurate."

BETTER FORECASTING

In many cases, a business can get better results by changing from one forecasting method to another. There are many success stories.

One of our military clients has obtained better results in predicting weapons systems failure rates by using methods based on the Weibull distribution instead of the binomial distribution. Another client, an automobile manufacturer, abandoned its exponential smoothing model in favor of Kalman filtering and achieved far more accurate forecasts. (All these terms are in the Glossary.)

Sometimes, however, the solution isn't this easy. We heard about a firm that sent fourteen of its managers to a week-long seminar on Box-Jenkins analysis at $1,995 a head. When they got back, they were nicely tanned and understood the method reasonably well, but they found that their offices looked different. While they were gone, the people who organized the seminar had also sold the firm a supermini-computer, several high-resolution graphics monitors and other peripheral devices, a lot of software, an in-house training course on how to use the new system, and a five-year maintenance contract.

The punch line: it turned out that ARIMA modeling had little to offer in that company's particular business situation. It yielded about the same level of accuracy that they had been getting all along by drawing a trend line on a sheet of paper. This was the point no one had thought to question.

Then again, you may be in a business where *no* forecasting method will work. We are honest enough to tell you that this can happen. Many small consulting firms, for example, get along fine without a forecasting system. Revenues fluctuate widely from one month to the next, and inventory control is not an issue—consulting services are shelved in the proprietor's head, and they do not spoil. In a period of peak demand, the staff puts in overtime, turns down new business, or possibly hires a temporary assistant with modeling experience.

You can waste a lot of time and money developing a time series model that fits your existing data beautifully. But if those data are subject to major perturbations from one source or another, the model may not give you accurate forecasts anyway.

CHOOSING A METHOD

We have said that there are three major categories of time series methods. Within these major groups there are dozens or hundreds of specific techniques, depending on who is counting.

The situation is not quite as bad as it sounds, because on closer inspection many of these techniques turn out to be minor variations of one another. A few methods can be thrown out if you have no resident mathematician, others because they are silly, and still others because there is no satisfactory commercial software with which to implement them. (The latter situation may change, of course, by the time our book is published.)

Besides, there is no law that says you have to adopt a single fore-casting method. Older books (some of them written since 1984) talk about the relative costs associated with each method, but this reasoning is largely obsolete. With a computer, it is just as easy and inexpensive to run several different models at once and compare the results later.

Some businesses, in fact, have a policy of running three different forecasting models simultaneously and then averaging the results. If sufficient historical data is available, the three estimates should be weighted to reflect the past reliability of each method.

There are a lot of methods, and you may not want to read about all of them. The decision table presented later in the chapter is designed to help you bypass the sections of the book that you will not need. But we encourage you to read all of it, because we went to a lot of trouble writing it.

Also, like any other book, ours builds on information contained in earlier sections. If you skip around you may miss some terms. For that reason, we have provided a highly detailed Glossary and Index. These are our favorite parts of any book.

DEMAND VS. SALES

Before selecting a method, you need to decide what you are trying to forecast. Most business forecasters are concerned with the volume of demand or sales or both. Volume, in turn, can be expressed in units or in dollars. (Throughout this book, unless specified otherwise, we are talking about sales volume in units.)

The demand for a product is usually defined as the number of units of the product sold during a forecast interval, plus the number back-ordered. But this definition underestimates actual demand, because it does not include customers who took their business else-where when the product was not in stock. By this definition, demand equals sales plus back-orders *plus* lost sales. In real life, this definition may be hard to implement, because information on lost sales may not be available. Forecasting usually means sales forecasting.

PATTERNS

The best forecasting method to use depends largely on three factors: what kind of data you have, how much of it you have, and what sort of pattern it follows. (Of course you won't know the exact pattern until after you have developed your model, but you should have a general idea after reading this section, based on your knowledge of your business.)

A series of data values may have any of four basic patterns: *horizontal, lumpy, trending,* or *cyclical.* It may also show a combination of two or more of these patterns.

Horizontal data remain at about the same level from one forecast interval to the next. The individual data values may vary a lot, but the average remains the same from year to year. This pattern is also called stationary, level, or flat. It makes forecasting either very easy or very hard, depending upon how much the data values fluctuate around the average:

- If there is a lot of variation, but it is random as far as you can tell, then the pattern is said to be *lumpy.* Time series analysis may not work in this case, so you are left with judgmental forecasting. (You can also try causal modeling if you think some outside events may be influencing the pattern, but then you have to figure out what they are.)

- If the data values fluctuate very little, then the pattern is said to be not lumpy. (We do not know of any special term for non-lumpy horizontal data.) Time series analysis should work in this case.

Trending data, when plotted on a graph, show a gradual pattern of increase or decrease over time—a trend, in other words. In order to see the trend, however, you may need to use some smoothing method such as regression. Even if the original scatter graph looks like a mass of dots, there could be a trend pattern hidden in there. After smoothing, the graph may look like a straight or curved line, or the rate of increase or decrease may change abruptly at some point. (Such a point is called a *turning point.*)

Cyclical data fluctuate according to a predictable pattern. In business applications, usually this pattern corresponds to the seasons or months of the year, so the pattern is often called *seasonal.* (There are also longer cycles, lasting several years or decades, but these are useful mainly to scientists or econometricians.)

The following criteria are often used in deciding whether a series of data values is seasonal or not:

- Sales must show a peak in the *same* season every year. Data values can fluctuate a lot without being truly seasonal. If the peaks are not predictable, you have a lumpy pattern instead.

- In order to meet the first test, obviously you have to look at data for more than one year. Most businesses require three years of data, unless it's an obvious seasonal product line, such as Christmas ornaments.

- Demand during the peak season must be significantly higher than demand during the rest of the year, not just slightly higher.

- Many companies also require that there be some identifiable *reason* for the peak before they decide that an item is seasonal.

You may find that not too many products survive all these tests of seasonality. Those that do, however, must be further classified as either *horizontal-seasonal* or *trend-seasonal*. The first type shows predictable peaks in demand over the course of a year, but overall demand stays about the same from one year to the next. Trend-seasonal demand combines a trend pattern with a seasonal pattern.

There are two different kinds of trend-seasonal models called *additive* and *multiplicative*. Figures 4-1 and 4-2 shows graphs that explain the difference. With additive seasonality, the peaks stay about the same height with respect to the trend line. If there is multiplicative seasonality, the peaks get bigger as the line trends uphill.

FORECAST HORIZON

Forecasting may be short-term, intermediate, or long-range. These terms refer to how far in the future you are trying to predict some event. Your choice of a forecasting method will depend partly on the forecast horizon of interest.

The horizon definitions vary from one book to another and from one company to another, but we are using the terms as follows:

- Short-term forecasting deals with events up to three months in the future. (Forecasts up to one month in the future sometimes are called "immediate term.")

- Intermediate forecasting refers to forecasting for a period of three months to two years in the future.

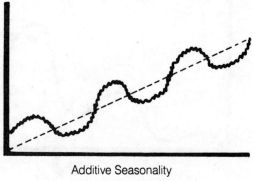

Additive Seasonality
Increasing Linear Trend

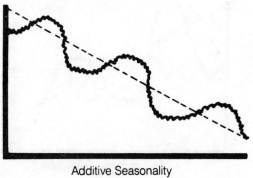

Additive Seasonality
Decreasing Linear Trend

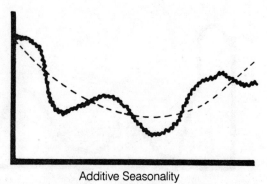

Additive Seasonality
Changing Trend

Fig. 4-1. Examples of Additive Trend-Seasonal Pattern.

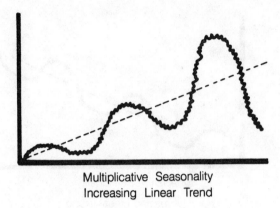

Multiplicative Seasonality
Increasing Linear Trend

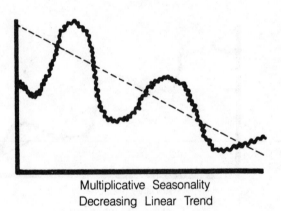

Multiplicative Seasonality
Decreasing Linear Trend

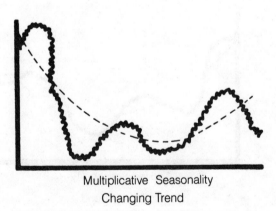

Multiplicative Seasonality
Changing Trend

Fig. 4-2. Examples of Multiplicative Trend-Seasonal Pattern.

- Long-range forecasting refers to events more than two years in the future.

This book focuses mainly on the short-term horizon, which is used for routine month-to-month sales forecasting. For anything beyond a few months to a year, time series methods tend not to work. (This statement also applies indirectly to causal models, because in order to use them for forecasting, you need to be able to predict future trends in the causal variables. Chapter 7 explains more about this.)

Long-term forecasting generally refers to econometric modeling, which is not covered in this book. Judgmental forecasting also makes use of anticipated long-term trends, as discussed in chapter 5.

The binary key in Table 4-1 should not be applied uncritically. If the key points to a mathematical technique, for example, this does not mean that you should disregard human judgment.

Table 4-1. Selecting a Short-Term Forecasting Method.

1a.	No numeric data history available—2.
1b.	Numeric data history available—3.
2a.	One person makes all decisions: *Good Guess*, Chapter 5.
2b.	Decentralized management: *Combined Forecast* methods, Chapter 5.
3a.	Causal factors known or suspected: *Simple Regression*, Chapter 7. *Multiple Regression*, Chapter 7. *MARMA*, Chapter 7.
3b.	Causal factors unknown or unknowable—4.
4a.	Data meets tests of seasonality—5.
4b.	Data not seasonal—6.
5a.	Simple regression reveals trend-seasonal—7.
5b.	Seasonal only, no trend: *Base Series Method*, Chapter 6. *Winters Method*, Chapter 6. *Spectral Analysis*, Chapter 6.
6a.	Simple regression reveals trend only—8.
6b.	Horizontal only: *Moving Average*, Chapter 6. *Exponential Smoothing*, Chapter 6. *Adaptive Filtering*, Chapter 6. *Box-Jenkins* (ARMA), Chapter 6.

Table 4-1 (cont.)

7a.   Additive seasonal pattern:
    Winters Method, Chapter 6.
    Spectral Analysis, Chapter 6.
    Box-Jenkins (SARIMA), Chapter 6.
    Decomposition, Chapter 6.
7b.   Multiplicative seasonal pattern:
    Winters Method, Chapter 6.
    Box-Jenkins (SARIMA), Chapter 6.
    Decomposition, Chapter 6.
8a.   Linear trend (or linear after transformation):
    Double Exponential Smoothing, Chapter 6.
    Trend Analysis (Simple Regression), Chapter 6.
    Box-Jenkins (ARIMA), Chapter 6.
8b.   Nonlinear trend (quadratic, etc.):
    Triple Exponential Smoothing, Chapter 6.
    Box-Jenkins (ARIMA), Chapter 6.

OTHER METHODS

Some forecasting methods discussed in our book do not fit neatly into Table 4-1. These methods are useful, but only under highly specific circumstances.

For example, suppose that you are not trying to predict a number, but the answer to a "yes-no" type of question. You want to develop a model to predict which customers will pay their bills, and which will not. Or which convicts released within the past year are likely to end up back in the slammer; or which consumers are likely to be interested in purchasing a heat pump.

Some definitions of forecasting exclude these types of questions, but we beg to differ. The questions pertain to the future, after all, and the methodology is practically the same. In a case like this, you might try a method called discriminant analysis. It is discussed in chapter 7, and it is nearly the same thing as multiple regression.

Another specific type of forecasting situation calls for a Markov chain. This is similar to a first-order autoregressive model—that is, a time series model which says that each number in a series of numbers influences the next one in the series. Autoregressive models are discussed in chapter 6. In business, however, the term "Markov chain" often is used in a more restricted sense to mean a simple method that requires only a pencil and paper. A simple example is presented in chapter 5.

DOING IT

After deciding on a method, the next step is deciding how to implement it. Each method requires its unique blend of data, people, hardware, software, time, and money.

Judgmental forecasting techniques, however complex they may sound on paper, involve little more than getting a bunch of people together and talking. (The main exception is the Delphi method, in which the participants write down their opinions without consulting one another.) These techniques are discussed in chapter 5.

Time series models, except for the very simplest ones, should always be implemented with the aid of a computer or programmable calculator. Chapter 6 tells you what the various methods do and how they work. Chapter 9 reviews some statistical software packages and tells which methods they include and how easy they are to use.

Causal models generally require more advance planning than time series models, because you have to decide which outside factors are likely to be influencing your data. In most cases, you will also need to locate some data regarding these outside factors. If you sell umbrellas, for example, you already have sales data, but you may also want to think about rain. Implementing the model will require a computer and the guidelines in chapters 7 and 9.

When you are using any forecasting method for the first time, often it is helpful to retain a forecasting consultant to answer everyone's questions, write or upgrade the documentation, and generally make the transition period easier. We can refer you to a good consultant if you are having trouble finding one.

SUMMARY

There are three major categories of forecasting techniques: judgmental, time series, and causal. The first is based on human judgment and the last two involve mathematical models. A model is a mathematical representation of a relationship between two or more events. A simulation is usually a mock-up of a real-life situation, designed to test the assumptions of a model.

A "good" forecasting method is one that works for your particular business situation. The chapter provides objective guidelines for selecting the most suitable method from those available. Some of the factors that influence your choice of model are the forecast horizon, the pattern of the data, and the type and amount of data available.

REVIEW QUESTIONS

1. Name the three types of forecasting models, as defined in this book. Which type of forecasting is used most often in your organization? Why do you think this is?

2. Distinguish between modeling and simulation.

3. Why do you think time series forecasting models tend not to work very far in the future? Can you think of situations in which this general rule might not apply?

ENDNOTES

1. H. R. White, *Sales Forecasting: Timesaving and Profit-Making Strategies That Work* (Glenview, Illinois: Scott, Foresman and Company, 1984), 9.

2. S. Waldman, and B. Roberts, 1988. "Grading Merit Pay." *Newsweek*, 14 November 1988, 45.

3. J. C. Compton, "Results of a Telephone Survey of Technical Documentation Users." *IEEE Transactions on Professional Communication*, December 1986, 93-99.

4. White, *Sales Forecasting: Timesaving and Profit-Making Strategies That Work* (Glenview, Illinois: Scott, Foresman and Company, 1984), 9.

5
Judgmental Forecasting

Hain't we got all the fools in town on our side? And ain't that a big enough majority in any town?

—Mark Twain, *Adventures of Huckleberry Finn*

This chapter introduces the reader to the following topics:

- The meaning of judgmental forecasting.

- The most common judgmental forecasting techniques.

- The relative advantages and disadvantages of judgmental vs. quantitative forecasting.

DEFINITION

Judgmental forecasting, also called subjective forecasting, is based mainly on human judgment rather than on mathematical models. The distinction sometimes is arbitrary, because judgment and mathematics are interrelated.

In many situations you will estimate numbers that you can't measure directly, by taking a survey or a good guess, and then you will use these numbers to do some further analysis. An example later in the chapter shows how this is done. In fact, you use judgment whenever you decide what variables to put into a model. And it works the other way around, too. The results of prior mathematical analysis may influence the forecaster's opinions. (At least one hopes that this is the case.)

Some judgmental forecasting techniques amount to pure guesswork, although this fact tends to be obscured by the formal discussions of theory and methodology presented in many textbooks. There is no need to apologize for human judgment, however, because in many situations it is the best (or only) forecasting method available.

In most judgmental forecasting techniques, an organization appoints one or more experienced staff members to predict some event of interest, such as the demand for refrigerators in the year 2000, or the future of the defense industry. Clearly, if this technique is to work, it requires a forecaster with a different set of skills than would be needed for developing a mathematical model.

VALIDITY

As we said, mathematical models are created, selected, and implemented on the basis of human judgment. Probably the reverse process takes place continually, too, in the sense that people's opinions are based on some form of mathematical reasoning that takes place without their awareness.

When you are driving home on the freeway at rush hour, for example, you have a pretty good idea of what time you will arrive. The reason is that past experience has enabled you to build a sort of model. Everyone has such models, and they tend to be fairly accurate. The authors, for example, generally can predict their own commuting times to within about 8%.

If you could see your commuting model, it might turn out to be something like multiple regression (chapter 7). The predictor variables that go into it might be traffic density, weather, any accidents announced on the radio, density of road construction workers, time of day, and day of the week. In other words, these are the factors you might think about when estimating your time of arrival.

But there are many other factors that you do not recognize or cannot monitor directly, such as wind resistance, the amount of carbon buildup in the engine, the mood of other drivers, or your own level of fatigue or eyestrain. These factors will be sources of unexplained variation in the model.

Like an overt mathematical model, this type of model is subject to manual override. If you have just won $100 in the lottery, you may throw out the model. You will feel capable of flying home on wings of light, and the estimate will fall short of reality.

Unfortunately, such a model is subject to what might be called data entry errors or sampling problems. Traffic density is hard to estimate by subjective means, for example, because by human standards it is always excessive. Following a recent commute, one of the authors was convinced that the average speed could not have exceeded five miles per hour. But the trip would have taken six hours, rather than the actual 80 minutes, had this estimate been correct.

DOES IT WORK?

Respected authorities in the field of forecasting have expressed divergent views on this subject. For example:

> Judgmental methods should not be viewed as "last resort" techniques . . . since in many situations they can provide more accurate forecasts than those derived from sophisticated mathematical models.[1]
> Forecasting users, that is, managers, must learn to rely much less on subjective methods. The evidence is overwhelming that human judgment does not necessarily improve accuracy over objective methods and it usually degrades that accuracy when routine, repetitive tasks are involved.[2]

These quotations may give the impression that forecasters are engaged in a fundamental debate as to the relative merits of judgmental vs. mathematical procedures. Suffice it to say that good forecasting requires both elements, and that good forecasters know this. Authors sometimes emphasize one viewpoint or the other for rhetorical purposes.

The best rule on this subject was developed not by the Harvard School of Business but by Charles Darwin, who once wrote: "General impressions are not to be trusted." But when Darwin wrote this, he was referring to any kind of data that can be counted or measured readily.

In other words, if you need to forecast the number of cars on the freeway next Wednesday, do not trust your feelings alone. Start counting cars. If you need to forecast customer demand for the new microprocessor-controlled butter curler that your company will introduce next year, go with your gut feelings. The product has no demand history, so there isn't anything to measure.

THE GOOD GUESS

In a business that consists of a single individual, a judgmental forecast amounts to a good guess. The same thing happens in a larger business if its future is largely dominated by the personality of one entrepreneur. This method is subject to the same range of outcomes as any other.

More often, however, judgmental forecasting is a group effort. The various methods are known collectively as combined forecasting and are discussed in the following paragraphs.

THE JURY OF EXECUTIVE OPINION

The JEO method really means that a group of executives get together and talk. They arrive at what is hoped to be a consensus opinion; but the rules governing group processes dictate that one or two individuals will dominate the meeting. The method then degenerates to the Good Guess procedure which we discussed earlier.

If the dominant individuals are also skilled at forecasting, of course, then a good forecast is likely to result. And if they don't know what they are doing, if they voice their hopes rather than their objective opinions, the outcome will reflect that fact as well.

The jury method is the forecasting technique most widely used by American businesses.[3] The reason is clear: It is essentially the same thing as a business meeting, so everyone understands how it works. It costs nothing, aside from the considerable amount of time involved, and requires no specialized equipment or software. On the negative side, it requires far more time and effort than statistical methods (on the order of ten times as much) and there is no clear evidence that it works better.[4]

Only 54% of managers in a recent survey were satisfied with this method and 22% were dissatisfied with it.[3] By contrast, the same survey showed that 67% of managers were satisfied with regression analysis and that only 14% were dissatisfied with it.

SALES FORCE FORECASTING

This method is the same as the jury of executive opinion, except that the meeting is composed of sales personnel rather than management. According to one study, more than 70% of businesses use this method and about half of them find the results reasonably accurate.[5]

Some salespeople forecast on the low side so that they will consistently exceed their quotas. Others take the opposite approach, predicting high sales volume in order to appear enthusiastic and positive. Every group consensus probably is based on a combination of the two strategies and they tend to cancel each other out.

THE DELPHI METHOD

> *It was six men of Indostan*
> *To learning much inclined,*
> *Who went to see the Elephant*
> *(Though all of them were blind)*. . .
> —J.G. Saxe, *The Blind Men and the Elephant*

The Delphi method, like the two previous methods, was not designed specifically for forecasting but lends itself to that application. It is simply another method for obtaining a consensus from members of a group. Presumably it was named for the famous Greek Oracle of Delphi. (The name has an unfortunate connotation, however, because the Oracle traditionally spoke in gibberish.)

Instead of meeting in one room, the participants in the Delphi method receive a questionnaire and complete it without consulting one another. The questionnaire asks for predictions regarding some specific events of interest to the company. In most cases, the participant is asked to include a reason for his or her answer.

After the results are tabulated by the person or agency conducting the study, they are returned to the participants for a second round of responses. Participants who expressed an unusual or dissenting opinion the first time are asked to justify it.

The Delphi method can be a very lengthy process, particularly if a large group of participants is involved. It can be more effective than the jury of executive opinion, because it avoids the bandwagon effect to some extent. Within a typical organization, however, no opinion is ever really anonymous. Participants may even feel intimidated by the fact that they have to write down their answers. For a review of this method, see reference.[6] According to Armstrong, the principal advantages of the Delphi method are that "It sounds fancy, yet the users can understand it."[7]

The success of this method, like that of any other subjective forecasting method, depends largely upon the knowledge and skill of the participants. Thus it also depends indirectly on the skill of the managers who *select* the participants.

As we said in chapter 1, studies have shown that the most successful forecasters often have formal training in forecasting. This general rule applies mainly to short-term sales forecasting, however, rather than to predictions of long-term econometric trends.

FINAL FORECAST

Down went the owners—greedy men whom hope of gain allured;
Oh, dry the starting tear, for they were heavily insured.
                                                    —William S. Gilbert

Many businesses do not rely on a forecast derived from any one method. They use one or more mathematical models to obtain objective forecasts, and prepare a weighted average of the results. They also use one or more committee methods in order to benefit from the wisdom of their executives and sales staff.

Then, the owner or chief executive officer examines the resulting composite forecast and uses his own intuition to override it if he finds it lacking. The result is called a final forecast.

ANALOGOUS DATA

A new product, or a new version of an existing product, has no sales history. Therefore, businesses typically forecast sales for such products on the basis of data for comparable products. Such data is said to be analogous or surrogate. This is a fine method, so long as the other product really is analogous to the one in question.

The analogous data method is not a judgmental forecasting method in itself. Judgment enters into the selection of the analogous product. Beyond that point, however, the same range of judgmental and mathematical techniques is available as in any other forecasting situation.

TECHNOLOGICAL FORECASTING

The name of this technique is somewhat misleading. It sounds as if it refers to a highly sophisticated method of forecasting which uses highly advanced technology, perhaps a Cray computer. In reality, it means a judgmental forecast that is based on considerations of current and projected trends *in technology*.

If a company wants to forecast demand for small, lightweight portable computers by the year 1995, for example, it might look at the new types of computer display screens which currently are being developed. Very small laptop computers have been around for years, but demand has been limited by the fact that the types of displays available, such as LCDs, are not entirely satisfactory. Once better displays with lower power consumption have been developed, the market for this product line is expected to take off.

Technological information can be used in conjunction with any of the subjective forecasting methods discussed in this chapter. Again, the technological approach is not a specific forecasting method in itself, but provides input to other methods.

CUSTOMER SURVEYS

A customer survey can be administered by telephone, by mail, or in person. It can be used in either of two ways: to estimate what your customers will do in the future, or to analyze the reasons for their past behavior.

If you want to know how many widgets a customer will buy from you next year, for example, it makes sense to ask him directly. But what if he doesn't know either?

Experience with surveys has revealed that the respondents tend to avoid giving negative-sounding answers.[8] Even if a respondent hates your products and does not intend to buy any next year, the chances are that he will not put it quite that way. He might say that his sales have been brisk and that he looks forward to seeing your spring catalog, when really he intends to swat flies with it.

Also, if your forecasting skills are limited, your customer's are not likely to be very much better. Perhaps he does not know how many widgets he will need next year. But he doesn't want to say that, because then it might appear that he does not know what he is doing. Or it might appear that the widget-based systems he manufactures are not moving very well. Therefore, he might tend to give you an estimate that is both hedged and somewhat inflated.

Given these limitations, you can still use survey data to good advantage. You can compare these data with the results of time series analysis and determine later which one worked better. Also, if you take a survey every year, you might be able to estimate the error factor involved (do clients tend to overestimate or underestimate future demand?).

CHAINING

Survey data also can be used in another way. Suppose, for example, that you have determined the total demand for a specific type of heat-resistant ceramic rings in the United States during 1990: $18 million. No advertising campaign is likely to increase the total market. Either a client needs ceramic rings or he doesn't.

Assume that your company makes Brand X ceramic rings. Your corporate goal is to carve off as large a share of this market as possible. As a forecaster, you can contribute to this goal in at least two ways:

• Using the classical time series methods described in chapter 6, you forecast future demand for the product in order to ensure adequate stock levels. This type of analysis is based solely on past data.

• Using a survey, you determine what percentage of customers will *switch* vendors each year, and which alternative vendor they are likely to choose, and why. This type of analysis is based on judgment (yours and your client's).

To continue the example: Your initial sales volume amounts to $7.2 million per year, or 40% of the market. Two other companies, Y and Z, make the same kind of rings and each has a market share of 30%.

So you take a survey and learn that, during each forecast period, 50% of customers switch brands. They are equally likely to switch to either of the two competing brands:

> Now using X: 50% loyal, 25% switch to Y, 25% switch to Z.
> Now using Y: 50% loyal, 25% switch to X, 25% switch to Z.
> Now using Z: 50% loyal, 25% switch to X, 25% switch to Y.

What will the market shares be in the next forecasting period? Well, let's start with Brand X. Its market share was 40%. Then it lost half of its business, or in other words 20% of the market. But it gained back *less* than the 20% that it lost, and here's why. First, it gained 25% of Y's market share, or 7.5% of the total market (0.25 × 0.30). Then it gained 25% of Z's market share, or 7.5% of the total market (0.25 × 0.30). The total gained was only 15%, so the new market share for Brand X is only 35%.

How about the others? Y started with 30% of the market and lost half of this. It also gained 25% of X's share (10%) and 25% of Z's share (7.5%). Y now has a market share of 32.5%. The same figures apply to Company Z.

This is a simple example of what is sometimes called a *Markov chain*. Markov was a mathematician, and the word "chain" refers to the fact that each set of probabilities (percentages) influences the next ones, like links in a chain. Or like an autoregressive time series model, as discussed in chapter 6.

You can see that the three companies will reach some sort of equilibrium within a few forecasting periods. Better lower the price on your rings—especially if you are selling them to the federal government—or else throw in some discount tickets to Disneyland. (But if you can come up with a mathematical model that predicts how these perks affect demand, then you have entered the realm of *causal* forecasting.)

So why isn't this example in chapter 6 with the time series models? Here we go with fuzzy classifications again. The method could be included in either chapter. But the way we see it, a time series model usually involves fitting a series of actual data values to some theoretical model, such as a straight line. This isn't what we did here.

In the Markov chain example, we did not have a series of actual data values. We had just one—the figure 50%—and we got it from a survey, rather than from direct observation. Then we generated a whole series of steps from it in a mechanical fashion. In other words, we did a sort of paper simulation. Meanwhile, back in the real world, that percentage could have been changing continually, or it might not have been valid in the first place.

Survey results need to be interpreted with care. When you make a forecast on the basis of your own past sales, you have direct access to the records. You might not know about all the perturbations that could arise, but at least you are starting with the right numbers. When you rely on survey results, however, you are dealing with a whole new set of assumptions—for example, that the busy manager who answers the phone is really interested in your problem and is giving you correct information.

Customer surveys can be extremely valuable, but only if they are carefully designed and skillfully administered. The wording of the questions and the identity of the interviewer often are crucial. Like statistical analysis, market research of this type often is best left to specialists.

SIMULATION

As we said in chapter 4, almost everything in life is a simulation from somebody's perspective. Some simulations take place in the physical world, others on paper, and others only in the human imagination.

The previous section on Markov chains included an example of a simple simulation. We set up some assumptions and then figured out what would happen if the assumptions were true. This is known as the *scenario* approach. It is used in cases where a physical simulation isn't possible.

Sometimes, however, more than one kind of simulation can be applied to the same problem. For example, suppose that an Army researcher has developed an equation to describe the rate at which harmful bacteria would spread through the atmosphere in the event of biological warfare. This is potentially a useful thing to know. But there has never been a full-scale war of this type, so there are no real data with which to test the model. And it would be inelegant to test it by actually starting a war, or by covertly dumping some deadly bacteria over one of our own cities.

In a case such as this, a simulation might be either computer-generated or physical. In the first case, a random number generator (a program that makes a series of unpredictable numbers) could be used to represent the error term in the model. The result would tell us where the bugs might end up, given certain assumptions about the prevailing winds and so on. This is an example of what is called a Monte Carlo simulation. (Businesses often use the Monte Carlo method, too, especially for things like predicting how long their customers will have to stand in line, given a certain number of grocery checkout stands. A computer program called GPSS is widely used for this purpose.)

In the second case, harmless bacteria or some kind of dye might be released, and the results would be measured and compared with those predicted by the model. The value of these simulations would depend, of course, on whether the behavior of the computer model, the harmless bugs, or the dye molecules was similar to that of the bacteria that would be used in a real war.

The physical type of simulation is less common in business, unless you stretch the definition a little. One possible example that comes to mind is the famous Orson Welles "War of the Worlds" scare in 1938. A lot of people bought train tickets, or guns, or simply gave their money to charity when they thought Martians had invaded the Earth. Okay, so it was an honest mistake. But it's possible that a business might stage a bogus disaster like this in order to see how it might affect sales. Every time there is an abrupt shortage or price increase for some commodity, some of us wonder if a simulation is in progress.

But here is a more mundane example. Suppose that your company is planning to introduce a new soft drink and you are not sure how well it will sell. You think you know, and so you have developed a model. To test the model, you need to sell some actual cans of soda. But marketing it nationwide would cost a lot of money, so at first you just introduce the product to one representative small town and see what happens. This is sort of a simulation, in that the town is made to represent the whole country. But it is basically the same thing as sampling.

Another type of simulation is known as role playing. Instead of simulating bugs or Martians or a population of 250 million consumers, you simulate a viewpoint. The executive or salesman pretends that he is his own customer. He might wear a costume and might even enter a kind of hypnotic state, in which he becomes convinced that he is the customer, and starts to behave like a prison guard or a plasma-coating engineer or an acne sufferer. Yes, grownups really do things like this.

Role playing is familiar to students of law, psychology, and political science, but it is less often implemented by business. Armstrong cites some examples.[9]

SUMMARY

Judgmental forecasting methods are based on human judgment rather than on mathematical models. The most common sources of information are (1) forecasters who express their opinions in a meeting, (2) forecasters who express their opinions separately, and (3) customer surveys. The information obtained by these methods can be subjected to further analysis through chaining or various simulation techniques. The effectiveness of these methods depends largely on the skill of the forecasters and on the quality of the available data.

REVIEW QUESTIONS

1. Is judgmental forecasting more effective or less effective than forecasting based on mathematical models? Explain your answer.

2. Which method discussed in this chapter (if any) would be appropriate for each of the following applications?

a. Forecasting sales of parts for a new automobile model.

b. Forecasting the retail price of optical disk drives for home computers as of 1992.

c. Forecasting next month's demand for turtle grooming brushes, based on five years of demand history.

3. Compare the jury of executive opinion and the Delphi method, stating the principal advantages and disadvantages of each.

ENDNOTES

1. G. Kress, *Practical Techniques of Business Forecasting: Fundamentals and Applications for Marketing, Production, and Financial Managers* (Westport, CT: Quorum Books, 1985). 151.

2. S. C. Wheelwright, and S. Makridakis. *Forecasting Methods for Management.* (New York: John Wiley, 1985), 365.

3. J. T. Mentzer and J. E. Cox, "Familiarity, Application and Performance of Sales Forecasting Techniques," *Journal of Forecasting* 3(1984):27-36.

4. V. A. Mabert, "Statistical Versus Sales Force-Executive Opinion Short Range Forecasts: A Time Series Analysis Case Study," Paper No. 487, Institute for Research in the Behavioral, Economic, and Management Sciences, Purdue University, 1974.

5. H. R. White, *Sales Forecasting: Timesaving and Profit-Making Strategies That Work* (Glenview, IL: Scott, Foresman and Company, 1974), 36-37.

6. H. Sackman, *Delphi Critique: Expert Opinion, Forecasting, and Group Process* (Lexington, MA: D. C. Heath, 1975).

7. J. S. Armstrong, *Long-Range Forecasting: From Crystal Ball to Computer.* (New York: John Wiley & Sons, 1985), 119.

8. J. C. Compton, "Results of a Telephone Survey of Technical Documentation Users." *IEEE Transactions on Professional Communication*, December, 1986, 93-99.

9. J. S. Armstrong, *Long-Range Forecasting: From Crystal Ball to Computer.* (New York: John Wiley & Sons, 1985), 124-132.

6
Time Series Models

Today is like yesterday and tomorrow.

—Neanderthal Man in *The Inheritors*
by William Golding

This chapter will introduce you to the following topics:

- The meaning of time series analysis.

- The advantages and disadvantages of time series analysis.

- The general characteristics of the most common time series forecasting models.

DEFINITION

The term *time series analysis*, like many other terms used in forecasting, has more than one connotation. Usually it refers to any mathematical method used to analyze time series data. Time series data, in
turn, means a series of values for some variable as measured at
equally spaced points in time.

By this definition, a lot of things qualify as time series analysis.
For example, if you look at all of your office telephone bills for the past
six or eight months and observe that each of them came within a few
dollars of $100.00, then it is reasonable to base next month's budget

on the assumption that the telephone bill will once again be about $100.00. Sure, this is mathematics. You have extrapolated a series of numbers. (If this does not seem sophisticated enough, you might go a step further and find the average of the six most recent bills, and use that as your forecast.)

To most academically trained statisticians, however, time series analysis has a more specific meaning. In this sense, there are two different kinds of time series analysis: the *frequency domain* approach, also called spectral or harmonic analysis, and the *time domain* approach, which includes the autoregressive model (see chapter 3) and Box-Jenkins analysis.

Our book uses the broader definition of time series analysis, because this is the definition that seems to be preferred by business forecasters. Limiting it to things like spectral analysis and autoregressive models would alienate most people, including us.

We should also point out that a time series model does not necessarily involve time. You might not have guessed this otherwise. For example, you might measure the thickness of a piece of thread at uniform intervals along its length in order to find some pattern in the variations. For purposes of analysis, this is basically the same thing as a time series.

ADVANTAGES OF TIME SERIES MODELS

The best of prophets of the future is the past.

—Lord Byron, *Journal*

Many types of data lend themselves to time series analysis. The main requirements are as follows:

- Accurate figures must be available for equally spaced points in time. Monthly telephone bills are a reasonable example of this type of data.

- A considerable *amount* of past data must be available. In the preceding example, it should be clear that telephone bills for only two successive months would not tell you very much, although they would be better than nothing.

- The data should follow some kind of pattern. If the monthly telephone bills for a year range from $14.00 to $2,667.00, for example, with no detectable trend or cyclic pattern, then time series analysis alone will not help you. (A causal or judgmental approach would be required in this instance.)

If these three conditions are met to a reasonable extent, then time series analysis offers an objective, often quite accurate forecasting method. And most time series methods are quite easy, especially with the help of a computer.

DISADVANTAGES OF TIME SERIES MODELS

It's a poor sort of memory that only works backwards.

—Lewis Carroll

What many people seem not to realize is that time series analysis is based *only* on what has happened in the past. Let us return to the example of forecasting your office telephone bill.

Again, suppose the bills for the past six months have averaged about $100.00. But you have hired a new temporary assistant who will arrive next week to help you during the rush season, which for your business is the month preceding Halloween. (You make computer-generated light shows for haunted houses or something.)

The assistant has just moved here from a distant state, where he is involved in a custody battle with his ex-wife, a lawsuit with his former employer, and a foreclosure on his house. He is likely to spend some time on the phone. Your phone bill is about to change. (This is an example of what is sometimes called a perturbation in the data.)

At this point, your time series model will fail. The model knows nothing about your new assistant, and it cannot write a memo ordering him to stop using the phone for personal calls. It knows only what you have told it. It will doggedly project the October telephone bill as $100.00, when in fact it might be closer to $500.00.

But wait. This does not imply that time series analysis cannot work on data that are subject to abrupt changes. All we are saying is that it cannot predict *unprecedented* changes. To continue this example, assume this is not the first time you have hired an October assistant. You have done the same thing every year for the past five years. If you have saved your bills for five years, you will note that they have averaged $100.00 for months other than October and $500.00 for October.

What does this mean? Are you a sucker for hard-luck cases? Do temporary employees take advantage of you? Or are *you* making most of those calls, because you are too busy in October to write letters?

In any case, now the time series model knows there will be a peak in October. It generates a forecast of $500.00. But when the real bill comes along, it is for $950! Apparently $500 was your normal rush season phone bill. Superimposed on this, you have the new guy's problems.

NAIVE MODEL

We will start with the simplest time series model that anybody actually uses, and then work our way on up.

According to the naive time series model, the next forecast interval will show no change from the previous forecast interval. This was how we took our first stab at predicting the phone bill. In other words, if the September telephone bill is $100.00, the October bill is assumed to be $100.00. If the October bill is $950.00, the model predicts that the November bill also will be $950.00, and so on.

The model is "naive" in the sense that it lacks information. Like Pinocchio, it uncritically accepts each new piece of information that comes along. In some books, this method is called last period forecasting or a random walk model. But it is not as bad as it sounds. Some forecasters claim it is the best model for predicting the stock market, and we will find some other uses for it later on.

The naive method will seem more impressive if you call it a random walk model and write it on a blackboard as follows:

$$\text{(Eqn. 6-1)} \quad Y_t = Y_{t-1} + e$$

Y is what we are calling the amount of the phone bill. The notation Y_t means "the value of Y at time t." So the equation says that the phone bill for month t will be the same as it was for the previous month, plus (or minus) a random error factor.

ARITHMETIC AVERAGE

By this method, the forecast is the average of all your past data values. If you have monthly sales figures for the past year, then you take the twelve values, add them up, and divide by twelve. The result is your forecast for next month.

The arithmetic average method can be satisfactory in the case of a truly horizontal pattern. It smooths out the random "lumps" in the data, if they aren't too large, and gives you a fairly good overall picture. But the arithmetic average doesn't work well at all if you have a trend or seasonal pattern.

As an example of a trend, suppose that sales volume has been increasing steadily for the past year. The average might give you some idea of what the demand was six months ago, but this is not what you want to know.

As an example of a seasonal pattern, let's assume that you sell an average of 500 widgets in December and 5 in every other month. This is November, and you want to make a forecast for December. So you find the average of the following numbers: 500, 5, 5, 5, 5, 5, 5, 5, 5, 5, 5, 5. The result is 46.25. (You can't sell part of a widget, so you round it up to the next whole number, 47.) You can see right away that this forecast is dead wrong.

Extra Credit Problem: Write an equation that represents the arithmetic average method, using the same kind of notation that we used in Equation 6-1. (You will need to use some letter such as n to represent the total number of months.)

MOVING AVERAGE

The naive model uses the data for just a single month. The arithmetic average method is based on the average of the data for all previous months. The moving average is a cross between these two methods: you find the average demand for just a *few* previous months.

This method was developed when people began to find that the arithmetic average method was impractical. If an item has been around for a long time, there might be so much demand history that you can't include all of it in the average. The older data probably is stored away in a box somewhere, and anyway it might not tell you much about present demand.

So you make an arbitrary decision as to where to stop. Perhaps you decide to use data for the previous year, or for the previous six months or three months. At that point, what you have is the moving average method. Unhappily, the term *moving averages*, or MA, is used in business forecasting to mean two quite different things. For the other definition, refer to the discussion of the Box-Jenkins technique later in this chapter.

The moving average method is widely used in business forecasting. One recent survey of managers showed that 85% were very familiar with this method, but only 58% were satisfied with its results and only 24% were using it for short-term forecasting. Even fewer used it for intermediate and long-range forecasts.[1]

But how do you decide how many months of data to use? And why is this very different from the naive model, or from the common-sense approach described at the beginning of this chapter?

- "Several" means any number of forecast intervals that the forecaster decides to use, most often three.* (If a smaller number is chosen, the model is said to be more sensitive to recent trends in the data. If a larger number is chosen, the model is said to be more stable.)

- The moving average technique is *not* very different from the naive model. In fact, if only two or three intervals of data are used, it is almost the same thing as the naive model.

- It is exactly the same as the common-sense approach, and therein lies its appeal.

But the moving average technique is not all bad. It can be used by anyone, and it does not require a computer. It can work fairly well if the data remain about the same from one forecast interval to the next, or if there is a gradual, steady trend of some sort. (In the latter case, you can use the linear moving average method, which just means taking the moving average of a series of moving averages. Got that?)

EXPONENTIAL SMOOTHING

There are many different versions of exponential smoothing (ES). In general, when we refer to ES, we mean the single method described in this section. For a review of many different forms of ES, see reference[2].

Exponential smoothing (ES) was developed in the late 1950s, when computers were expensive and slow and had only a limited amount of memory. The method was good in those days because the calculations are simpler than those required for regression. Also, ES doesn't require the computer to store very much data.

This is no longer an important concern, because computers have improved a lot. Even if all you have is a personal computer, you can buy a 30-megabyte hard disk for a couple of hundred bucks—or a gigabyte optical disk for somewhat more money—and store all the data you want on it. But many businesses continue to use exponential smooth-

---

*The popularity of the number three has no mathematical significance. It has more to do with the way human beings view the world. In fact, this is probably why there are three kinds of forecasting models.

ing anyway, even for trending data, because it works fairly well and everyone is familiar with it.

As of 1982, 73% of surveyed businesses were familiar with the exponential smoothing method, 60% were satisfied with it, and 24% used it for short-term forecasting.[2] It was less often used for longer forecast horizons.

This section, unlike most of the book, will show you actual numbers and calculations. There are two reasons. First, we want to show you what life will be like if you decide to forecast without a computer. Second, there are probably some forecasters in some smaller organizations out there who really *can't* get access to a computer. ES is about the most complex method you should tackle without one.

The most important thing to know about exponential smoothing is that it is *not* a shortcut way of doing regression, as some books claim. ES is very much like the moving average method. The only difference is that ES uses a *weighted* average. (We talked about weighted averages in chapter 3.)

First let's recap the other methods we have covered so far, using the following twelve months of data:

$$14, 22, 20, 26, 13, 18, 35, 17, 16, 28, 24, 19$$

At this point, we suggest that you get out a calculator (or a pencil and paper) and see if you agree with the following results:

- By the naive (last period) method, the forecast for next month would be 19.

- By the arithmetic average method, the forecast for next month would be 21.

- By the moving average method, using the last three months of data, the forecast for next month would be 24 (23.67 rounded up).

These three methods are alike except for the number of months of data they use. But as you can see, the number of months can make a big difference in the forecast. Using three different methods, we obtained three different numbers: 19, 21, and 24.

Now judgment enters the picture. If you have some reason to believe that the recent demand figures are important, and that the earlier ones aren't, then you might base your forecast on one month of data, or three months, or six months. If you feel that all of the demand history is equally important, then you would use all of it. With these methods, the values that you decide to use have equal importance, and the ones you throw out (if any) have zero importance.

Exponential smoothing provides a sort of compromise between keeping old data and throwing it out. It assumes that the most recent demand history has the most importance—but it also assumes that the earlier data has *some* importance. The older the data, the less value it has for predicting the future.

This sounds reasonable. But how do you express "importance" in terms of numbers? One common way is to assign a weight to each of the past data values. As we explained in chapter 3, weights are just fractional numbers that add up to 1. A data value that gets a high weight will have a strong influence on the way the average turns out. A data value that gets a low weight will have less effect.

Weighted averages seem like cheating to many people. After all, if these weights are just pulled out of thin air, you can make the forecast come out any way you want. Right you are! This is done all the time in business. It is important to use a good method for selecting the weights, so that the result isn't just plain fudging. As you read more about forecasting, you will find that most of the different forecasting methods amount to different people's ideas of how to find the best weights.

Exponential smoothing isn't necessarily the best way to select these weights. But it is a fairly good way, and it is widely accepted in business, so it is a good method to learn. Remember that a computer can do all the tedious calculations shown here. You won't have to do them by hand.

SMOOTHING CONSTANT

In order to do exponential smoothing, you have to tell most computer programs what *smoothing constant* to use in the calculations. The smoothing constant also is referred to by the Greek letter alpha (α) or by the English (or Roman) letter a.

You will see how alpha is used once we get to the examples. It has to do with how fast the forecast will respond to changes in demand. The higher the value of alpha, the more weight is assigned to the recent data, and the less weight the older data will get.

The value of alpha might sound like a hard thing to decide, but it isn't. In practice, alpha almost always is between 0.1 and 0.6. The best value—the one that yields the most accurate forecast—can be found by trial and error, and usually it turns out to be 0.1 or 0.2 for horizontal data. Some computer programs, such as FORECAST PRO, will automatically find the optimal value for the smoothing constant.

Such programs also enable you to override this option and specify a value if you prefer.

DATA PATTERNS AND ES

Exponential smoothing can be used with all three of the basic patterns: horizontal, trend, and seasonal.

If there is no trend in the data, the method is called *single* exponential smoothing. The resulting forecast is called a single smoothed value, or SSV for short. This is the most common form of exponential smoothing.

Suppose that you sell blenders and other small kitchen appliances. It is December 1984 and you want to calculate a forecast for each of your product lines for January 1985. First, you need to multiply each of the past sales figures by its weight. For the alpha value, 0.2 is a good value to start with. You can always change it later if the results are not satisfactory. The weights are calculated as follows:

Month	Formula for Weight	Weight	
December	a	.2	
November	$a(1-a)$	.16	
October	$a(1-a)^2$	.128	
September	$a(1-a)^3$	.102	
August	$a(1-a)^4$	.082	
July	$a(1-a)^5$	.066	
June	$a(1-a)^6$	.052	
May	$a(1-a)^7$	.042	
April	$a(1-a)^8$	.034	
March	$a(1-a)^9$	.027	
February	$a(1-a)^{10}$	.022	
January	$a(1-a)^{11}$	.017	. . . and so on.

The months are listed in reverse order because you start with the most recent forecast interval, which was December 1984.

You can see that these weights are getting smaller and smaller. Now you can see why it is called exponential smoothing. For each successively earlier forecast interval, the exponent gets bigger and the weight gets smaller. If you plotted all these weights on a graph, they would form an exponential curve.

We stopped after twelve months, in order to avoid boring you too much. But you can see what is happening. The weights are starting to get close to zero, so those earliest months of sales history aren't going to count for much in calculating the forecast.

For the example, we will use the same data values as before. This time they represent sales of garbage disposals:

14, 22, 20, 26, 13, 18, 35, 17, 16, 28, 24, 19

If you multiply each one of these numbers by its weight, you will get the following:

Sales	Weight	Product
19	0.2	3.8
24	0.16	3.84
28	0.128	3.58
16	0.102	1.63
17	0.082	1.39
35	0.066	2.31
18	0.052	0.94
13	0.042	0.55
26	0.034	0.88
20	0.027	0.54
22	0.022	0.48
14	0.017	0.24
	TOTAL	20.18

You might guess that the last column total, 20.18, is the January 1985 forecast. But it isn't, because we stopped after only twelve months of data. The weights are supposed to add up to 1, but so far they add up to only 0.93. This means we have calculated only about 93% of the forecast value.

To get the forecast, then, we divide 20.18 by 0.93. The result is 21.7. (Instead of using this shortcut, you could continue the calculations for another six months or a year of data, as the computer would do. But this is a lot of work, and besides, you might not have that much data available.)

You may have noticed that this forecast, 21.7, is not much different from the forecast we got by the simple arithmetic average method, which was 21. In fact, the single smoothed value and the arithmetic average are always the same number, *if* you have a lot of data *and* if there is no trend in it.

So far, we have done an awful lot of calculations. Some shortcut method! But in the old days, this method actually saved a lot of computer time and storage space. The reason was that the computer didn't need to store the data or repeat the calculations every month. It just saved the old forecast each month and *updated* it as new data came in. This is the same thing you will probably want to do if you are using a pencil and paper.

To update the forecast, you "smooth" the current month's sales into the old forecast:

Next month's SSV forecast =
(0.2)(current sales) + (0.8)(last month's SSV forecast)

The alpha value is 0.2, so the fraction 0.8 represents (1 − a).

DOUBLE EXPONENTIAL SMOOTHING

If it looks as if there might be a trend in the data, but you aren't sure, then the first thing you need to do is to use the simple regression model to find out whether there is a real trend or not. Regression is an option in almost every statistics program. As a shortcut, you might draw a graph of the data and look for an obvious trend.

If you find that there is a trend, the single smoothed value won't be able to keep up with it. To get more accurate results under these conditions, you need to use a different method. One of these—not necessarily the best, but certainly the most familiar—is called *linear* or *double exponential smoothing*.

You start out exactly the same way as before. First, you find the single smoothed forecast for January 1985 by going through all the steps shown in the previous section. Then you do the same for February 1985, and so on until (say) another year has passed. Now you have a list of twelve SSV forecasts.

If you take those twelve SSV forecasts and do exponential smoothing on *them*, the result is called a *double smoothed value* or *DSV*. But the DSV itself is not the forecast. As the example in this section will show, the forecast will be equal to 2 times the current SSV minus the DSV.

This technique baffles many people, because it sounds as if you can't start double smoothing right away. You have to wait several months or a year until you have enough single smoothed forecasts to use in calculating a double smoothed value. This is true, at least by the method shown here, but it makes sense when you think about it. In order to use single exponential smoothing, or any other method, first you need to have a certain amount of data to put into the formula. In this case, the data consists of old SSV forecasts.

Let's start where we left off, with the January 1985 forecast equal to 21.7. Now that a year of sales data is available, you begin to suspect that there is an upward trend. Therefore, you decide to use double smoothing.

You can't wait another whole year to start double smoothing, so you decide to fudge and wait only six months. The data values for January through June 1985 are shown in the following table. Real life is different from a classroom; you get to decide how much data you will use. Just remember that less data means less accurate results.

	Month	SSV	Weight	Total
	June	33.5	.2	6.70
	May	30.6	.16	4.90
	April	28.3	.128	3.62
	March	26.4	.102	2.69
	February	23.7	.082	1.94
1985	January	21.7	.066	1.43
	Total		.738	21.28

In order to get the first DSV, for July 1985, we multiplied the six SSV forecasts by the first six weights that we used before. The sum of those six weights is 0.738. Again, the weights need to add up to 1.0, so the total must be divided by 0.738 to get the double smoothed value:

$$21.28 / (0.738) = 28.8$$

The next step is to calculate what is called the *trend adjustment*, by subtracting this double smoothed value, 28.8, from the current SSV, which is 35.2 (see Table 6-1). The result is 6.4. You add this trend adjustment to the current SSV. The total, 41.6, is the trend adjusted forecast shown in Table 6-1 for July 1985.

You might have noticed that there is a quicker way to do this. There was no real need to go through the step of calculating a trend adjustment. If you multiply the current SSV forecast by 2, and then subtract the DSV, you will get the same result, 41.6. We showed you how to do it the hard way so you would know what a trend adjustment is.

Finally, to calculate the double smoothed value for August and later months, you use the following shortcut formula. Again, alpha = 0.2. (These DSVs do *not* include the trend adjustment.)

New DSV = (.2)(New SSV Forecast) + (.8)(Old DSV)

Table 6-1. Example of Trend-Adjusted Forecast.

Month	Actual Demand	SSV	DSV	Trend Adjusted Forecast
August	41	36.4	30.3	42.5
July	44	35.2	28.8	41.6
June	42	33.5	—	—
May	45	30.6	—	—
April	40	28.3	—	—
March	36	26.4	—	—
February	37	23.7	—	—
1985 January	32	21.7	—	—
December	19	—	—	—
November	24	—	—	—
October	28	—	—	—
September	16	—	—	—
August	17	—	—	—
July	35	—	—	—
June	18	—	—	—
May	13	—	—	—
April	26	—	—	—
March	20	—	—	—
February	22	—	—	—
1984 January	14	—	—	—

By this formula, the DSV for August is $(.2)(36.4) + (.8)(28.8) =$ 30.3. To get the trend adjusted forecast for August, multiply the SSV by 2 and subtract the DSV, just as you did before: $(2)(36.4) - 30.3 =$ 42.5, the forecast that appears in the table.

In order to make it clear where these values come from, Table 6-1 repeats all the data used in the examples. The blank spaces in the table result from the fact that, by this method, the SSV values could not be found until twelve months of data were available. Similarly, the DSV calculations could not start until we had six months of SSVs.

In order to simplify these examples, we used the same smoothing constant (0.2) for double smoothing as for single smoothing. Some forecasters believe it is better to use a lower smoothing constant for double smoothing. One rule of thumb is that the alpha for double smoothing should be one-half of that for single smoothing. You might try repeating the calculations, using an alpha value of 0.1 for the double smoothing step.

TRIPLE SMOOTHING

With the preceding method, the trend adjusted forecasts may lag behind actual sales if there is an unrecognized *quadratic* trend in the data. This just means a pattern of geometric or exponential growth or decline. Instead of being straight, such a trend line curves upward or downward very quickly. You can read more about this in chapter 3.

In this situation, the appropriate model may be triple (or quadratic) exponential smoothing. If you liked double smoothing, you'll love triple smoothing. You can probably guess how it is done. When you had a series of SSVs, you smoothed them to get DSVs and then found the trend adjusted forecast. By the same token, you can take a series of DSVs and smooth them to get TSVs. This gets a little bit tedious, and you should use a forecasting program to do it.

HOLT'S TWO-PARAMETER SMOOTHING

This is another variation of exponential smoothing which can be applied to data with a trend. The formula involves a second parameter, called beta (β), in addition to the smoothing factor alpha. It is preferable to double smoothing in many situations, especially if the trend line is curved rather than linear.

The Holt procedure is somewhat complex, and we will not work through an example here. If you want to use this method, try a program such as STATGRAPHICS, STATPAC GOLD, or FORECAST PRO. The latter program can calculate values for both smoothing constants. Some other programs require you to select these values yourself.

Linear exponential smoothing methods rarely produce the exact same forecast values as least squares regression, but the answers should be fairly close. If your data shows a trend pattern, try both methods and see which works better.

For example, we took the data from Figure 3-2 in chapter 3 and applied both Holt's method (with parameters optimized by FORECAST PRO) and least squares regression. The Holt method gave a forecast of 142.16; least squares produced the value 146.62. In actual use, these would probably be rounded to 142 and 147 respectively. The Holt method resulted in an R^2 value of 0.48 and an adjusted R^2 of 0.376. With least squares, the unadjusted R^2 value was about 0.62.

THE SEASONAL INDEX METHOD

If you are still with us, then you are really committed to exponential smoothing. But if you look at an example of seasonal data, you can see that ES alone won't suffice—double, triple, or quadruple. You need a procedure for dealing with periods of peak demand. The simplest method is called the seasonal or base index method.

You are a small appliance dealer again, and here are five years of demand history for fruitcake presses:

	Jan	Feb	Mar	Apr	May	Jun	Jul	Aug	Sep	Oct	Nov	Dec
1981:	4	5	6	5	4	5	5	6	4	5	7	496
1982:	6	6	4	4	5	6	5	4	6	6	5	501
1983:	5	4	5	6	6	4	4	5	5	4	5	498
1984:	6	6	5	6	5	5	6	5	6	4	4	507
1985:	4	4	5	4	5	5	5	5	4	6	4	498

Fruitcake presses, unlike garbage disposals, seem to be a hot Christmas item. We have five years of data, so we can be fairly sure that this pattern is consistent. The average demand for December is 500, and the average demand for months other than December is 5. We want to calculate a forecast for January 1986.

First, we will try single exponential smoothing with three different alpha values: 0.1, 0.2, and 0.3. We will spare you the calculations and just summarize the results:

Alpha	SSV Forecast for January
0.1	73.4
0.2	110.7
0.3	154.8

As you can see from these numbers, SSV forecasts are worthless when the pattern of demand is seasonal. The real data shows that January demand has never been outside the range 4 through 6. None of the forecasts even comes close to this range.

The easiest way to get around this problem is to calculate what is called a base index (abbreviated BI) or seasonal index. This method, like almost everything else in statistics, translates into what common sense would tell you to do anyway:

1. Accumulate at least three years of data. You can't tell what the seasonal pattern is if you have data for only one year. (You might get away with two years.)

2. Find the average sales for each month of the year. For December, for example, add up the five December values in the table

and divide the total by 5. Repeat for each of the other months. In our data, the average of sales for December turns out to be 500 and the average for each of the other months is 5.

3. Find the average sales for *all* months, by adding them all up and dividing by the number of months. In this case, the 60 values sum up to 2775, so the average is 2775/60 or 46.25. This last number is called the *deseasonalized sales* or DES. (If you are thinking in terms of demand instead of sales, you call it the DED.)

4. If you take the average sales for a given month, and divide it by the DES, the resulting number is the *base index* for that month. If the base index is greater than 1, it means sales volume is relatively high that month. If the base index is less than 1, it means sales are down. Note that the sum of all twelve base indices must equal 12.

In our data, the base index for December is:

$$500 / 46.25 = 10.8$$

For each of the other months, the base index is:

$$5 / 46.25 = 0.11$$

The January 1986 forecast is equal to the DES times the base index for January, or

$$(46.25)(0.11) = 5.1$$

The result would have been exactly 5.0, except that we rounded some of the numbers. This result is just what common sense would predict, since the average demand for January has been 5. It seems like a lot of trouble, though, doesn't it?

In fact, if you look carefully at what we did, it might even seem silly. All we did was to find the January average, divide it by the DES, and then multiply the result times the DES again! The only possible result was the original January average. But, this is the way the base index method is used.

The method starts to be useful only when there is a *change* in sales volume. Then you need to update the DES by exponential smoothing. The base index also is updated once a year, as we will show.

A SUDDEN CHANGE IN DEMAND

Demand for a product can change unexpectedly. Suppose that it is the end of November 1986. Now you have sales data on fruitcake presses for five years plus eleven months. You want to predict sales for the next forecast interval, which is December 1986:

	Jan	Feb	Mar	Apr	May	Jun	Jul	Aug	Sep	Oct	Nov	Dec
1986:	12	9	8	10	11	13	8	10	11	9	9	—

Before you do any calculations, try common sense. You can see that sales volume has doubled. In past years, you sold about five presses per month during the off season. Now you are selling about ten. You might guess that sales for December 1986 also will be about twice what it was before. It was 500 before, so maybe it will be about 1000.

By the base index method, the first thing you do with the new data is to deseasonalize it. You do this by dividing each number by the base index for that month. You will use these values to update the DES each month.

The previous example shows that the base index for each off-season month is 0.11. Thus, the DES for January 1986 is 12/(0.11) or 109.1. You do the same for each of the other months.

But now that you have more data, the base indices themselves also need to be updated, so that you will have new ones to use next year. The base index for each month is updated once a year, each time there is a new sales figure to update it with. This step uses exponential smoothing with a relatively *high* alpha value (0.4 in this example).

Several steps are performed each month in order to update the DES and the base indices. We will explain these steps by using January as an example.

1. Find the current DES by dividing the January sales by the old January base index: 12/(0.11) = 109.1.

2. Smooth this DES into the old DES (46.25), using an alpha value of 0.2. As shown in Table 6-2, the result is 58.8.

3. To get the current base index, divide the current sales, 12, by this updated DES.

4. Smooth this new base index into the old one, using an alpha of 0.4.

These operations and their results are summarized in Table 6-2. To get the DES values next year, you will use the new base indices that are shown in the table.

Table 6-2. Updating the DES and Base Indices

January	(.2)(109.1)	+	(.8) (46.25)		=	58.8
	Current BI	=	12 / 58.8		=	0.20
	Updated BI	=	(.4)(.20) + (.6) (.11)		=	.15
February	(.2) (81.8)	+	(.8) (58.8)		=	63.4
	Current BI	=	9 / 63.4		=	0.14
	Updated BI	=	(.4) (.14) + (.6) (.15)		=	.15
March	(.2) (72.7)	+	(.8) (63.4)		=	65.3
	Current BI	=	8 / 65.3		=	0.12
	Updated BI	=	(.4) (.12) + (.6) (.15)		=	.14
April	(.2) (90.9)	+	(.8) (65.3)		=	70.4
	Current BI	=	10 / 70.4		=	0.14
	Updated BI	=	(.4) (.14) + (.6) (.14)		=	.14
May	(.2) (100.0)	+	(.8) (70.4)		=	76.3
	Current BI	=	11 / 76.3		=	0.14
	Updated BI	=	(.4) (.14) + (.6) (.14)		=	.14
June	(.2) (118.2)	+	(.8) (76.3)		=	84.7
	Current BI	=	13 / 84.7		=	0.15
	Updated BI	=	(.4) (.15) + (.6) (.14)		=	.14
July	(.2) (72.7)	+	(.8) (84.7)		=	82.3
	Current BI	=	8 / 82.3		=	0.10
	Updated BI	=	(.4) (.10) + (.6) (.14)		=	.12
August	(.2) (90.9)	+	(.8) (82.3)		=	84.0
	Current BI	=	10 / 84.0		=	0.12
	Updated BI	=	(.4) (.12) + (.6) (.12)		=	.12
September	(.2) (100.0)	+	(.8) (84.0)		=	87.2
	Current BI	=	11 / 87.2		=	0.13
	Updated BI	=	(.4) (.13) + (.6) (.12)		=	.12
October	(.2) (81.8)	+	(.8) (87.2)		=	86.1
	Current BI	=	9 / 86.1		=	0.11
	Updated BI	=	(.4) (.11) + (.6) (.12)		=	.12

Table 6-2 (cont.)

November	(.2) (81.8)	+	(.8) (86.1)		=	85.2
	Current BI	=	9 / 85.2		=	0.11
	Updated BI	=	(.4) (.11) + (.6) (.12)	=		.12

Now, to find the December forecast, take this new DES from Table 6-2 and multiply it by 10.8, the December base index that you calculated before:

$$(85.2)(10.8) = 920.16$$

The result is a bit lower than the 1000 we predicted by guesswork, but it is not too far off. So why did we bother with half an hour of calculations? Let's press on.

Now suppose that it is New Year's Day, 1987. The *actual* sales figure for December turns out to be 983, not 920 as predicted. Now you can update the December base index for future use:

Current BI   = Current Sales/New DES = 983/85.2 = 11.5
New BI   = (.4)(Current BI) +   (.6)(Old BI)
            = (.4)(11.5) +   (.6)(10.8) = 11.1

The December base index is about the same as it was before. This reflects the fact that, once again, about 100 times as many fruitcake presses were sold in December as in any other month.

TREND-SEASONAL DATA

There are several different ways to approach data that combines both a trend *and* a seasonal pattern. Only one of these methods is simple enough to do on paper, and then only if you have a lot of paper. It combines exponential smoothing, regression, and the base index method.

We do hope you are absorbing the intended message: This is both risky, in terms of accuracy, and a waste of your valuable time. You would not consider lighting your office with candles. For many of the same reasons, you should not do your forecasting on the back of an envelope. But let's continue, anyway.

In our previous example, demand increased in the sixth year. An increase sounds like the same thing as a trend, so you might wonder why we didn't treat it as one. The reason was that the increase was not *continuous*. Demand stayed the same for five years and then suddenly doubled. After it doubled, it remained at the new level. The techniques used for forecasting trend-seasonal demand do not work under those conditions, so we had to treat it as horizontal-seasonal.

The following table shows five years of sales data for programmable blenders. This product shows a trend-seasonal pattern. There is a peak in December each year, because this is an obvious gift item. But it's less exaggerated than in the previous example, because people have birthdays and anniversaries and weddings all year long. In addition, the overall sales volume is increasing as more and more people learn programming.

	Jan	Feb	Mar	Apr	May	Jun	Jul	Aug	Sep	Oct	Nov	Dec
1981:	4	7	6	9	8	12	13	10	16	15	16	41
1982:	17	13	15	18	20	21	20	27	27	29	30	63
1983:	26	22	28	32	37	30	38	40	39	42	44	92
1984:	40	39	47	49	43	50	52	55	60	58	62	127
1985:	59	62	66	64	63	70	72	76	71	80	87	189

We start by calculating a base index for each month, just as we did with the horizontal-seasonal data. But the method is slightly different this time, because we can't use the overall average in our calculations. The average doesn't mean much if there is a trend in the data.

In order to find the BI, we need to divide the sales for the month by some number that represents the "middle" of all the data for the year. (This is not a very technical way of putting it, but it describes what we are trying to say.) By comparing the month's sales with the "middle" sales, you can find out whether demand for that month is higher or lower than expected.

With horizontal data, the average is a good way of describing the middle. But we can't use the average this time, because it keeps changing, so we need to substitute something else.

What a trend really means is that the middle of the data keeps moving in one direction or the other, as sales volume gradually increases or decreases. When you move a point, you get a line. So this time you need a *line* to describe where the middle is. With trend-seasonal data, the base index for a month is the actual sales for that month divided by the corresponding point on the regression line.

You don't need to draw a picture of an actual line. You can represent it as an equation instead and save a lot of space. So we took the five years of data values that we showed you before and punched them into a statistical program. (If you insist, you can do it by hand, using the formulas in chapter 3.) The result turns out to be:

$$Y = -2.067 + 1.475X$$

As an example of how this formula is used, let's find the expected sales for month 14 (which means February 1982):

$$Y = -2.067 + (1.475)(14) = 18.58$$

But the *actual* sales for that month was 13. The base index for February 1982 is 13 divided by 18.58, or 0.70.

To get the overall February base index, find the February base index for each of the five years and then average them:

1981: $Y = -2.067 + (1.475)(2) = 0.88$
$BI = 7/.88 = 7.95$
1982: $Y = -2.067 + (1.475)(14) = 18.58$
$BI = 13/18.58 = 0.70$
1983: $5Y = -2.067 + (1.475)(26) = 36.28$
$BI = 22/36.28 = 0.61$
1984: $Y = -2.067 + (1.475)(38) = 53.98$
$BI = 39/53.98 = 0.72$
1985: $Y = -2.067 + (1.475)(50) = 71.68$
$BI = 62/71.68 = 0.86$

The average of these five base index values is 2.17, so it appears that this is the overall February base index.

But wait a minute. Judgment tells us that this result is dead wrong. For the last four years, 1982 through 1985, the actual February demand was *lower* than predicted by the regression line. Yet we have come up with a base index of 2.17, which means that February demand is more than twice as *high* as expected!

This looks bad, but regression is not the culprit. It is us. If we had looked carefully at the data, we would have noticed that the sales figures for early 1981 were very small. Any prediction involving very small numbers is suspect.

In this case, the base index for February 1981 was very high. It was high just because the numbers happened to be small, not because of any unusual sales activity that month. Only about six more items were sold that month than predicted, but this made the base index turn out very large. So when we added it in with the rest of the base indices, it threw the average off.

To fix this, we can do what is called kludging. We go back and calculate a new regression line, this time using only the first *three* years of data. (You will see where we are headed in a moment.) This time, the equation of the line turns out as follows:

$$Y = 2.218 + 1.284X$$

Next, we recompute the base indices for the first three years. They will be different this time, of course, because the equation is different:

1981: $Y = 2.218 + (1.284)(2) = 4.79$
   $BI = 7/4.79 = 1.46$
1982: $Y = 2.218 + (1.284)(14) = 20.19$
   $BI = 13/20.19 = 0.64$
1983: $Y = 2.218 + (1.284)(26) = 35.60$
   $BI = 22/35.60 = 0.62$

Average base index = $(1.46 + 0.64 + 0.62)/3 = 0.91$

Now this looks more reasonable. The February 1981 base index still is a bit high, but nothing like what it was before. And as we add the data for 1984, 1985, and later years, we will use exponential smoothing to update the February base index, with a fairly high smoothing constant of 0.4. This will give more weight to the recent base indices, and will tend to make the earliest ones go away.

As the first step in the updating process, we need to find the regression equation for the first *four* years of data. In other words, we will add in another year of data. The equation turns out to be:

$$Y = 0.918 + 1.338X$$

Using this equation, the expected sales for February 1984 (the 38th month in the table) are:

$$Y = 0.918 + (1.338)(38) = 51.76$$

The actual sales for that month were 39, so the February 1984 base index is 39 divided by 51.76, or 0.75.

Now we can smooth this base index into the old one, using an alpha value of 0.4:

New BI = (0.4)(Current BI) + (0.6)(Old BI)
   = (0.4)(0.75) + (0.6)(0.91) = 0.85

We continue this updating process by adding in the data for 1985. Now the regression equation is the same one we calculated earlier, when we were using all five years of data:

$$Y = -2.067 + 1.475X$$

This means the expected sales for February 1985 (month 50 in the series) are equal to:

$$Y = -2.067 + (1.475)(50) = 71.68$$

The actual sales volume is 62, so the current February base index is 62 divided by 71.68, or 0.86.

Again, we need to smooth this base index into the old one, using an alpha value of 0.4:

New Feb. BI = (0.4)(Current Feb. BI) + (0.6)(Old Feb. BI)
         = (0.4)(0.86) + (0.6)(0.85) = *0.85*

As you can see, this is a much more reasonable result than we got when we looked at the whole five years at once. We have shown you how to arrive at a reasonable-sounding base index for a single month, February. You would use the same process to get all the other base indices.

You can use this February base index to calculate a forecast for February 1986. First, you project the February value using any appropriate trend model, such as simple regression. Then you multiply the result by the base index of 0.85, in order to correct it for seasonality. The result is your forecast.

If you are not sure what happened or how we did this, you should read through the explanation again. (Either that, or skip it.)

SPECTRAL ANALYSIS

The base index method described in the previous section is the simplest way to handle seasonal data. It's about as far as you can go on paper, unless you are a real whiz. With the aid of a computer, however, you can use several more sophisticated seasonal models that might, in some cases, generate better forecasts. Spectral analysis is one of these methods. Another, called SARIMA, is discussed later in the section on Box-Jenkins analysis.

The term spectral analysis has nothing to do with ghosts or the supernatural. Instead, it comes from the word *spectrum*, meaning a range of frequencies. It refers to a group of frequency domain methods that are used for modeling cyclic data. The seasons of the calendar year form the most important cycle for many businesses, but there are other types of cycles as well.

UFO sightings are more frequent on Wednesdays; sunspots peak in frequency every eleven years or so; chipmunk population levels rise and fall. If you shut someone in a dark room, he switches over to a 25-hour circadian rhythm and keeps waking up later and later every morning. Women, like grunion, respond to the call of the moon. Come to think of it, when people talk about cycles they almost always come up with weird examples like this. Armstrong's happy phrase: "Spectral analysis is a dance in a different dimension."[3]

Harrison's harmonic smoothing method is a spectral analysis technique that is commonly used in business forecasting. It is appropriate for seasonal data with no trend, or in cases of *additive* seasonality. For a multiplicative seasonal pattern, you should use the Winters method instead (next section).

STATPAC GOLD and BMDP are two well-known statistical programs that can be used for spectral analysis. The formulas are too complex for presentation in a book that we promised would be nonmathematical. We will tell you, however, that these models involve the sine and cosine functions. As you may remember from trigonometry, a graph of one of these functions looks like a wavy line. Harmonic smoothing takes advantage of the fact that the graph of a seasonal event looks the same way.

WINTERS METHOD

This variation of exponential smoothing was developed by a statistician named P. R. Winters. It is an effective method for seasonal data, especially if a multiplicative pattern is present. We recommend that you try the Winters method on your computer if your data series appears to be highly seasonal.

The Winters method is similar to the Holt method that we discussed earlier in the chapter, except that a third parameter called gamma (γ) has been added to the model to represent seasonality. Selecting appropriate values for these three parameters can be a formidable task, but some programs such as FORECAST PRO calculate the best values automatically.

ADAPTIVE FORECASTING

The word *adaptive* implies that a forecasting model changes as it goes along, to take advantage of the most recent data. Exponential smoothing could be regarded as a simple example of adaptive forecasting, because the most recent data always gets the highest weight. Usually, however, the term is restricted to a group of techniques known as adaptive filtering.

Adaptive filtering was developed in the 1940s, primarily as a mathematical tool for engineering problems. Since the 1960s, however, these methods have also been applied to specific business forecasting situations with a high degree of success. The AEP technique, for example, was originally developed for real estate appraisal.[4] We have seen adaptive filtering used successfully for a variety of purposes, from predicting the error term in the pointing of a telescope to forecasting demand for automotive parts.

In 1977, Dr. Spyros Makridakis wrote:

> It is the author's opinion that filtering techniques are the most promising of time-series methods and that their usage will increase in the future and eventually pass to disciplines other than engineering.[5]

Despite this enthusiastic endorsement, adaptive filtering has not caught on very widely. Of the thirteen business forecasting programs reviewed in chapter 9, only STATPAC GOLD includes adaptive filtering as an option—and it doesn't say very much about the method, except to warn the reader that it can yield serious errors. (It can, of course, if used improperly.) Most of the published surveys of business forecasting methods don't even mention adaptive filtering, so we do not know what percentage of businesses are using it.[6,7]

The problem, in our opinion, is that adaptive filtering has not been made really accessible to the typical business manager. It is unfamiliar and sounds hard to use, and so it tends to stay that way.

Three variations of adaptive filtering used in business forecasting are AEP (adaptive estimation procedure), GAF (generalized adaptive filtering), and Kalman filtering.[4,8] In all these techniques, the weights are not arbitrary as in exponential smoothing, but instead are determined by some iterative process that tries to optimize them.

You need to designate an initial set of weights and a learning constant, generally symbolized by K, which determines how fast the program determines the best set of weights. Depending on the software, you might enter these values manually or else let the program select the values automatically.

DECOMPOSITION

Some of the most widely used business forecasting methods were developed by the U.S. Bureau of the Census. Taking a census is a big job, especially if you have to do it by hand. Once you have collected all that data, you need to be able to use it to predict various population trends.

The earliest of these Census methods was called Census I. We will not review it in detail here, because it is basically a manual system of computing 12-month moving averages. Census II is a computer program that you can buy from the Bureau of the Census. The same procedure also is included in several commercial forecasting programs, as discussed in chapter 9. At the time this book is being written, the latest version available is called X-11. There is also a quarterly version called Q-11.

X-11 is a refined version of a general technique called decomposition, which tries to break down a time series into four components: trend, seasonal, cyclical, and irregular. According to one survey, 42% of business managers were very familiar with decomposition and 55% of them were satisfied with it. But only 13% actually used it for intermediate forecasts, and even fewer used it for short-term and long-term forecasts.[2]

In X-11, you input the sales data—or whatever it is that you are trying to forecast—and decide how many months of data should go into the moving averages. Usually five months are used at first. Then the program calculates seasonal indices, makes adjustments for any fluctuations in sales that you might anticipate, and prints the forecast estimates for next year.[9]

SIMPLE TIME SERIES REGRESSION

A simple time series regression model, as defined here, is one in which the independent (X) variable is time. Chapter 3 describes how least squares works. It also explains the difference between this model and the autoregressive model, which is discussed later in the Box-Jenkins section.

First, we need to back up a little and explain some other ways of doing "regression." We will not try to unravel all the linguistic confusion that surrounds this term.* As used by business forecasters, the term regression includes all possible ways to draw a line through some points on a graph.

In this sense, there are three major types of regression—just as there are three major types of everything. We will call them freehand, semiaverage, and least squares.

---

*We received a resume from an applicant who claimed to have considerable experience in regression. When we asked what type, she replied, "Past lives." This is considered a satisfactory answer in California.

We note, however, that a recent survey questionnaire listed the following as three separate forecasting methods:[2]

- Regression
- Trend Line Analysis
- Straight Line Projection

We think we understand what the investigators meant. In this context, "regression" probably indicated a causal model. "Trend line analysis" usually means a mathematical regression in which the X variable is time. "Straight line projection" also sounds like a time series method. It might have referred to the freehand or semiaverage method, or both. But if we had to stop and scratch our heads, some of the survey respondents probably did, too. This is one potential problem with surveys.

Trend line analysis, then—which we think is the same thing as we are describing in this section—was used by 21 to 28% of businesses as of 1982. Straight line projection was used by 10 to 16%. In both cases, the higher figure represents the intermediate forecast horizon.[2]

The three major regression methods, by our definitions, work as follows:

- Freehand regression simply means that you plot the data on a scatter diagram and then try to draw a line by hand through the middle of the data points. This is not a very good technique. It works if the points nearly follow a straight line in the first place, or if only a low level of accuracy is required.

- The semiaverage method sounds much fancier than it really is. You start with a scatter diagram and then divide it down the middle, as shown in the following figure:

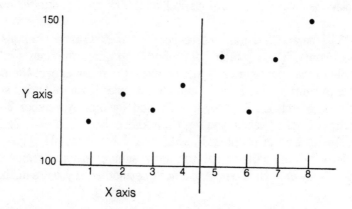

Next, you find the average of all the Y values to the left of this vertical line, and make (for instance) a red dot on the graph where this
value occurs. Then you find the average of all the Y values to the right
of the vertical line, and make another red dot. Finally, you connect the
two red dots, and this is your regression line. This also is pretty poor.
It can work if the data values are very uniformly distributed, but real
data values never are.

- The final method, least squares regression, is the one we mean by
  regression, and the one we will talk about for the remainder of the
  section.

As we stated in chapter 3, the equation for a straight line looks like
this:

$$(\text{Eqn. 3-3}) \quad Y = a + bX + e$$

The formulas for calculating a and b also are in chapter 3. This is very
tedious if you have to do it by hand—so don't. Any computer can be
used to perform the calculations, and many programs will even draw
the graph. Still, you should know what is going on.

In trend line analysis, X is time and Y is the thing that you are trying to predict—such as the number of units of a product which you will
sell at a given time. The letter e is the error term, which you can
ignore for now. The regression coefficient b is the slope of the line,
and a is the point at which the line would cross the Y axis on a graph if
the line went all the way across.

To use the formula, first you take all the past data values that you
have and feed them to your regression program. The values of X will
be points in time, and you need to represent them as numbers: 1, 2, 3,
and so on. (Some programs, such as ECSTATIC and STATPAC GOLD,
have a built-in variable that does this for you.) The program will then
display the values of a and b, as well as the R^2 value and other useful
information.

The data values must correspond to *uniform* time intervals. In
other words, if you switch from monthly to quarterly figures in the
middle of the year, you can't just combine them and expect the computer to figure it out. Here is another example: If you recorded some
event on March 12, July 20, July 23, and again on November 2, the
results will not be valid if you represent these dates as $X = 1, 2, 3, 4$.

As we said in chapter 3, when you use the simple regression
model with time series data, you are assuming that the values of Y
depend only on X and do not influence one another. If you are mistaken

about this, then you might get misleading results. But the model is often used as an intermediate step in forecasting—for example, as a quick check to see whether data has a significant trend or not. We used it this way when we were talking about exponential smoothing. In this context, the accuracy of the results might not be as crucial.

MAN VERSUS MACHINE

Is least squares regression really better than freehand regression? If you feel sure that a soulless machine cannot possibly fit a regression line as well as you can do it with a ruler, then you are not alone. Many businessmen and engineers feel this way.

In offices all over the world, collections of data points serve as Rorschach tests on which managers project their hopes and dreams. With a bit of creative interpretation, a graph that resembles a shotgun blast can be smoothed into any desired shape. Data points that do not fit the desired regression line can be ruthlessly pruned away.

If you show your boss what she wants, the short-term result might be a happy boss. The long-term result, however, might be a poor forecast and reduced profits. This is one instance in which a mathematical technique almost invariably works better than human judgment in discovering real trends in the data.

So we will try all three regression techniques with some sample data. These numbers could represent virtually anything, such as monthly sales of some product:

14, 27, 29, 17, 20, 19, 25, 37, 30, 31, 42

The results are shown in Fig. 6-1. The first graph represents one person's attempt to draw a freehand regression line through these data points; someone else would get a slightly different line. The second graph was produced by the semiaverage method, and the third graph by least squares regression.

The point of this exercise and the illustrations is that the line produced by least squares regression (Fig. 6-1c) looks at least as good as the others. Drawing this line, however, required no judgment or effort at all. Using MICROSTAT (a program reviewed in chapter 9) for the first time, it took us 45 seconds to read the menu, create and name a data file, type in the twelve numbers, ask for a regression and scatter plot, and get the results on the screen.

Once you have gotten a regression line, by whatever means, you can use it to project the forecast for a future time period. You just

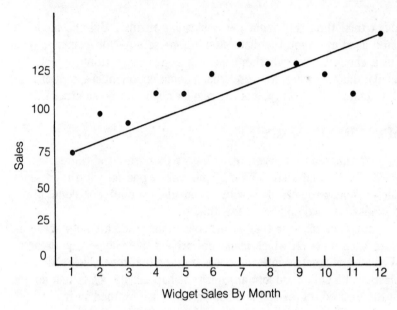

Y   =   85.91 + 4.67x
Data: 75, 100, 90, 110, 110, 125, 140, 130, 130, 125, 110, 150

Fig. 6-1a. Scatter Plot With Regression Line, Freehand Method.

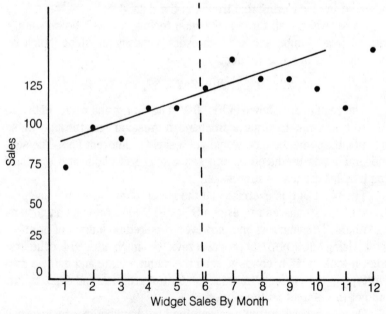

Y   =   85.91 + 4.67x
Data: 75, 100, 90, 110, 110, 125, 140, 130, 130, 125, 110, 150

Fig. 6-1b. Scatter Plot With Regression Line, Semiaverage Method.

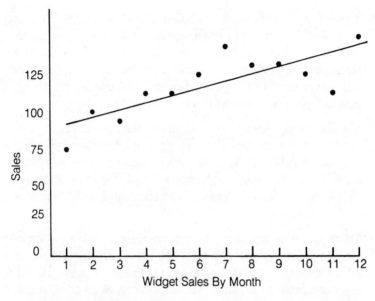

Y   =   85.91 + 4.67x
Data: 75, 100, 90, 110, 110, 125, 140, 130, 130, 125, 110, 150

Fig. 6-1c. Scatter Plot With Regression Line, Least Squares Method.

extend the line (if you are doing it freehand), or plug a future value of X into the equation. In this particular example, if you want a forecast for month 13, you calculate it as follows:

$$Y = 85.91 + 4.67X = 85.91 + (4.67)(13) = 146.62$$

LIMITATIONS

Trend line analysis, like anything else, has its pitfalls. When using it, you need to keep a few rules in mind. This is a good example of why you need to understand something about statistics before using a forecasting software package.

Some of these rules have already been mentioned, but we will summarize them here.

- Trend line analysis is of little use unless there is a measurable trend in the data. If there is no trend, use one of the simpler smoothing models.

- The trend must be *linear*. That is, the line that best fits the data must be a straight line. If this is not the case, you need to transform the data to make it linear. Most forecasting programs enable you to check for linearity and transform the data if necessary.

- Trend line analysis is not effective unless you have a reasonable amount of data. You can run a regression program even if you have only two or three data points, but the results will have little or no predictive value. Forecasters have proposed various rules of thumb: you need nine points, you need twenty-two points, and so on. The best guideline is to use as much data as possible.

- The simple regression model assumes that the values of Y are independent of one another. If this is not true, then the confidence level might be inflated, so that the model appears to be significant but isn't. Most statistical programs will test for autocorrelation and transform the data if necessary. The procedure is too complicated to explain here.

- Trend line analysis—like other time series methods— cannot be used to predict values very *far* in the future. A graph such as Fig. 6-1c, for example, is valid for the span of time indicated on the X axis. It's reasonable to assume that the same general trend might continue for a while. But the trend could turn right around in the next forecast interval. The most elegant demonstration of this fact comes not from Fourier or Gauss, but from Mark Twain.[10] This is the kind of quotation that you save for years, just waiting for an excuse to use it in a book:

> In the space of one hundred and seventy-six years the Lower Mississippi has shortened itself two hundred and forty-two miles. That is an average of a trifle over one mile and a third per year. Therefore . . . seven hundred and forty-two years from now the Lower Mississippi will be only a mile and three-quarters long, and Cairo and New Orleans will have joined their streets together, and be plodding comfortably along under a single mayor and a mutual board of aldermen.

BOX-JENKINS TECHNIQUE

Men are most apt to believe what they least understand.

—Montaigne, *Essays*

The Box-Jenkins technique has become something of a bandwagon, a rare phenomenon in the staid world of statistics. Since Box and Jenkins introduced their method in about 1970, other statisticians and business forecasters have written literally millions of words about it.[11] Part of the mystique of this method lies in the fact that few people can understand it.

Many academic statisticians believe, with some justification, that the Box-Jenkins technique is the best approach to time series analysis. As of 1982, however, only about 6% of American businesses were actually using this method. Sixty-five percent of survey respondents were completely unfamiliar with Box-Jenkins and 57% were dissatisfied with it.[1]

With reference to Box-Jenkins, Wheelwright states that "the method is difficult to understand and apply and frequently performs badly."[12] In a famous, much-debated debate, a group of statisticians ran into problems when applying the Box-Jenkins method.[13] One textbook author describes Box-Jenkins as an expanded version of exponential smoothing, which leads one to suspect that he might not understand it either.

Armstrong puts the matter succinctly:

> . . . it does not strike me as a good idea to use a complex method that you do not understand, especially when comparable results can be achieved with simple models that people do understand.[14]

What is wrong here? Are the goals of academic statisticians and business executives really that different? Is anything really that hard to understand? We will explore these issues in this section, and you can decide for yourself whether you want to use Box-Jenkins or not.

We will begin with three statements that might help to demystify this technique:

- Box-Jenkins is *not*, in itself, a forecasting model. It is a procedure for *selecting* an appropriate time series forecasting model.

- Box-Jenkins is valuable if you have a lot of time series data—say, for 40 to 50 forecast intervals—and if these data appear to follow some fairly stable pattern that you need to be able to predict. (The method would be a waste of time if you had, say, two years of quarterly sales figures and they showed a simple linear trend.)

- Box-Jenkins, like most things, can be extremely complicated if you insist on understanding all the nuts and bolts. But most forecasters don't need to understand it on this level, because you can't do it by hand anyway. Some computer programs ask you to make a few decisions about the data. Others do the whole job automatically.

The Box-Jenkins approach assumes that there are three different categories of time series regression models:

- Autoregressive (AR). As we said in chapter 3, this means a regression model in which there is correlation between successive values of the data. Some AR models are similar to a Markov chain (chapter 5).

- Moving average (MA). This does not mean the same thing that it did earlier in the chapter. The Box-Jenkins MA model is based on a moving average of past random *errors*. In other words, the model assumes that there is correlation between successive values of the error term.

- A combination of AR and MA (ARMA). In practice, it turns out that most data sets are best described by a mixed ARMA model.

Within each of these three categories, models are further described by parameters called p and q. These letters represent the *order* of the model, which just means the number of terms in the model. In chapter 3, we explained that the AR model could include all of the past values of Y or just a specified number of past values. This is what is meant by the number of terms. For example, this is a first-order AR model:

$$Y_t = b_1 y_{t-1} + e_t$$

Next we will show you a first-order MA model, in which the future value of Y depends on a function of the *error* term for the previous time period. We are using B rather than b here to distinguish between the coefficients for the AR term and those for the MA term. The minus sign in front of the B doesn't mean anything in particular, but it is conventional to use it:

$$Y_t = -B_1 e_{t-1} + e_t$$

An AR(p) model means an autoregressive model of order p, and an MA(q) model means a moving average model of order q. In the first example, then, p would equal 1. In the second example, q would equal 1.

An ARMA model combines these two models, so we would refer to an ARMA (p,q) model. Again, we aren't expecting you to calculate anything. We just want to be sure that you and your computer program are speaking the same language. An ARMA model with $p = 1$ and $q = 1$ would look like this:

$$Y_t = b_{11} Y_{t-1} - B_1 e_{t-1} + e_t$$

If the data values are seasonal, there are also two other parameters to worry about: P and Q, the seasonal values of p and q. These values are determined mainly on the basis of trial and error, but are usually equal to 0 or 1. Such models are called SAR, SMA, SARMA, and so on.

All of these models assume that past data values are horizontal (stationary), so it is necessary to remove any trend in the data by a process called *differencing*. A Box-Jenkins program will perform this step for you. A model using differenced data is called ARI, IMA, or ARIMA (the I stands for integrated). An ARIMA model is described by three parameters (p,d,q).

The term ARIMA is widely used as a synonym for Box-Jenkins, even by some authors who should know better. In reality, there are other ways to develop an ARIMA model. The name refers to an under-lying pattern in a time series, not the technique used to discover it.

With most programs, you select the category and order of the model on the basis of some values that the computer displays on the screen. This is the step that confuses most people, including many statisticians. Wheelwright offers some general guidelines for selecting a model, which we will paraphrase:

- Look at the autocorrelations, which probably are labelled on the graph that the computer displays. If they drop off exponentially to zero, the model is AR.

- Look at the *partial* autocorrelations, which also will be labelled. (We will not explain what these are; just look at them, and don't ask.) If they drop off exponentially to zero, the model is MA.

- If both the autocorrelations and partial autocorrelations drop off exponentially to zero, the model is ARMA.

- The order of the model, whether AR or MA or mixed, is the number of partial autocorrelations that are significantly different from zero.[15]

The rest of the process is largely automated. The program will use the resulting model to calculate a forecast.

If you are completely baffled at this point you might be pleased to learn that some new microcomputer software programs can perform *all* the steps of the Box-Jenkins process automatically. One of these, FORECAST PRO, is reviewed briefly in chapter 9. References [16] and [17] describe other automated Box-Jenkins programs. But you should still understand how the method works, because the method produces strange results if you abuse it.

Other programs that offer the Box-Jenkins method, with less automation but various degrees of online assistance, also are reviewed in chapter 9 of this book and listed in reference[18].

WHAT THIS MEANS IN REAL LIFE

I pass with relief from the tossing sea of Cause and Theory to the firm ground of Result and Fact.

—Sir Winston Churchill

Some concrete examples may help to clarify what we mean by an autoregressive model. In an earlier chapter, we noted that small consulting firms sometimes give up on extrapolative forecasting methods because of the lumpy pattern of sales. In many cases, however, such a firm could benefit from an AR or ARMA model. Our basis for this statement is as follows.

Getting a consulting contract takes a certain amount of time. You must call prospective clients, write proposals, wait for evaluations, and so on. For the sake of the example, let us assume that three months of lead time are required to get a new contract; that an average contract lasts six months; and that your firm has only three consultants and no marketing personnel.

A good rule is never to turn down a contract, as long as the work is legal and pays well. The number of hours in a day, however, is invariant. Therefore, your available time fills up first with work. If any time is left, for example at 3 AM, you can allocate it to marketing. If no time is left, however, you do no marketing during that interval.

You can see what will happen here. If there is a three-month lag between the beginning of a marketing effort and the beginning of a new contract, then your fortunes will tend to oscillate. When you are very busy doing work for clients, you will spend less time marketing. Three months later, a dip in revenues will result. The dip will be especially pronounced when it happens to coincide with the end of the longer six-month cycle which represents the conclusion of an assignment.

Conversely, when you are less busy, you will do more marketing. Three months later, a peak in revenues will result. And when this peak happens to coincide with the beginning of a six-month cycle, then all hell will break loose, and you will be working around the clock trying to catch up.

This is oversimplified, of course, but the principle is valid. We are describing an AR model, in which earlier values of Y influence later ones with a specific lag interval. Most businesses experience this phenomenon to some extent. It is probably less pronounced in larger businesses, however, because they experience numerous peaks and dips which tend to cancel one another out, resulting in a smoother curve.

(They also have sales and marketing departments that do nothing else.)

The MA type of model could be a little harder to visualize intuitively. Hoff aptly describes the model as follows:

> The moving-average concept is an interesting one, since it implies that any series value is really only a byproduct of past random errors. This conclusion makes sense, however, if you think of the random errors as small "shocks" that initially set the process in motion and continue to keep it in motion thereafter.[19]

In our AR example, there was the implicit assumption that it could have been set up as a causal model instead. That is, once you figured out where the cyclic pattern was coming from, you could have developed a formula to predict revenues in terms of hours of marketing effort or something. The MA model, by contrast, assumes that the perturbations that cause the lag effects are *random* events that could not be predicted by a causal model.

To continue the same example, consider the fact that your marketing effort will not always be uniformly successful. Sometimes you hit the jackpot, and sometimes you bomb out. In other words, sometimes there will be a peak in revenues that was *not* preceded three months earlier by a dip in revenues that, in turn, allowed more marketing. Sometimes, the peak will be preceded three months earlier by nothing more remarkable than a run of good luck.

This is where the MA term comes in. In real life, this kind of situation probably would require an ARMA model. Or an ARIMA model, assuming an upward trend in your fortunes. Or a SARIMA model, especially if much of your work comes from the government, which spends its money primarily at the beginning and end of its fiscal year. Or a SMARIMA model, assuming that you want to bring some causal variables into the act, too (see chapter 7).

So this is why many consultants—including forecasting consultants—do not develop forecasting models for their own business. Like a dentist who does not brush his own teeth, they reason that the length of a day is fixed. If they spent part of it developing and testing a highly complex model, they would have even less time for marketing. Does this sound familiar?

PARZEN'S ARARMA TECHNIQUE

ARARMA is similar to Box-Jenkins in that it is a technique for selecting a time series regression model. The name stands for autoregressive autoregressive moving average. AR is repeated because the method allows for two different kinds of time series, nonstationary and stationary, both of which might be modeled by AR terms.

The chief advantage of ARARMA is said to be the fact that it can be programmed to run without human intervention. It is true that FORECAST PRO and similar programs run Box-Jenkins analysis in a fully automated mode, but they achieve this result by means of an *expert system*—that is, by emulating a human forecaster's approach to Box-Jenkins. With ARARMA, a simple mathematical algorithm is supposed to handle these steps and several potential sources of error are thus eliminated.

Unfortunately, we were unable to find any microcomputer software that uses ARARMA, at least by that name, and it is unlikely that you will want to do it by hand. See references 20 and 21 for more information regarding this promising method.

SUMMARY

Time series analysis means (1) any quantitative method used to analyze time series data, or (2) least squares regression analysis as applied to time series data. A time series is a series of values for some variable as measured at equally spaced points in time.

REVIEW QUESTIONS

1. What is a time series model?

2. Is least squares analysis a time series model? Explain your answer.

3. Explain the difference between regression and correlation.

4. If the Box-Jenkins method is the best general approach to time series analysis, why doesn't everyone use it?

ENDNOTES

1. J. T. Mentzer, and J. E. Cox, Jr., "Familiarity, Application, and Performance of Sales Forecasting Techniques," *Journal of Forecasting* 3(1984):27-36.

2. E. S. Gardner, Jr., "Exponential Smoothing—The State of the Art: Extrapolative Methods," *Journal of Forecasting* 4(1985):1-38.

3. J. S. Armstrong, *Long-Range Forecasting: From Crystal Ball to Computer* (New York: John Wiley & Sons, 1985), 180

4. R. Carbone, R. Bilongo, P. Piat-Corson, and S. Nadeau, "AEP Filtering," chapter 6 in *The Forecasting Accuracy of Major Time Series Methods*, by S. Makridakis et al. (New York: John Wiley & Sons, 1984).

5. S. Makridakis, and S. C. Wheelwright, *Interactive Forecasting*, edited by C. Doerr (Palo Alto, CA: The Scientific Press, 1974), 23.

6. J. T. Mentzer, and J. E. Cox, Jr., "Familiarity, Application, and Performance of Sales Forecasting Techniques," *Journal of Forecasting* 3(1984):27-36.

7. H. R. White, *Sales Forecasting: Timesaving and Profit-Making Strategies That Work* (Glenview, Illinois: Scott, Foresman and Company. 1984).

8. R. K. Mehra, "Kalman Filters and Their Applications to Forecasting," S. Makridakis, and S. C. Wheelwright, edited by *Forecasting. Studies in the Management Sciences*, Volume 12, (Amsterdam: North-Holland Publishing Company, 1979), 75-94.

9. H. R. White, *Sales Forecasting: Timesaving and Profit-Making Strategies That Work* (Glenview, Illinois: Scott, Foresman and Company, 1984).

10. Mark Twain, *Life on the Mississippi*. (New York: Harper & Brothers, 1874).

11. G. E. P. Box, and G. M. Jenkins, *Time-Series Analysis* (San Francisco: Holden-Day, 1976).

12. Wheelwright and Makridakis, *Forecasting Methods for Management* (1985), 352.

13. C. Chatfield, and D. L. Prothero, "Box-Jenkins Seasonal Forecasting Problems in a Case Study," *Journal of the Royal Statistical Society: Series A*, 136(1973):295-352.

14. J. S. Armstrong, *Long-Range Forecasting: From Crystal Ball to Computer*. (New York: John Wiley & Sons, 1985), 175.

15. Wheelwright and Makridakis, *Forecasting Methods for Management* (1985), 120.

16. G. Hill, and R. Fildes, "The Accuracy of Extrapolation Methods: An Automatic Box-Jenkins Package (SIFT)," *Journal of Forecasting* (1984) 3(1984): 319-323.

17. G. Libert, "The M-Competition With a Fully Automatic Box-Jenkins Procedure," *Journal of Forecasting* 3(1984):325-328.

18. J. C. Hoff, *A Practical Guide to Box-Jenkins Forecasting*. (Belmont, CA: Lifetime Learning Publications, 1983), 300.

19. *Ibid.*, 51.

20. E. Parzen, "ARARMA Models for Time Series Analysis and Forecasting," *Journal of Forecasting* 1(1982):66-82.

21. A. C. Harvey, "A Unified View of Statistical Forecasting," *Journal of Forecasting* 3(1984):245-275.

7
Causal Models

If you can't prove what you want to prove, demonstrate something else and pretend that they are the same thing. In the daze that follows the collision of statistics with the human mind, hardly anyone will notice the difference.

—Darryl Huff, *How to Lie With Statistics*

This chapter will introduce you to the following topics:

- The reasons for using causal forecasting models.
- The use of regression in causal forecasting.
- The principles of multiple regression.

DEFINITION

Causal forecasting models assume that it is possible to identify factors that *cause* certain business trends, or other events of interest. Time series analysis, by contrast, looks at trends that occur over time.

To many readers, this may seem like academic hair-splitting of the worst sort. A simple regression model looks exactly the same, whether X represents time or the Dow-Jones Average. We often think of time as "causing" things to happen, particularly when buying new tires or wrinkle cream. But the statistician doesn't see it that way. As time advances, the values of other variables just sort of change along with it.

There are other differences between time series and causal models. You no longer have such a problem with autoregression; it is replaced by new concerns with names of similar length and obscurity. Also, with causal models, you might not be trying to project future values. Often you are just trying to define the relationship between two things, so that you can manipulate one of the things. (The purist might say this is not really forecasting, but we feel that it qualifies. Any forecasting method influences the future to some extent.)

In causal forecasting, often you will use several different X variables in the same model. Again, you can't do this in a time series model, because the universe has just one time line that we know about. Some kinds of models, however, include both time and causal factors as independent variables.

Many books include judgmental forecasting under the heading of causal methods, because judgment is based largely on perception of cause and effect. In our book, however, judgmental forecasting is treated separately in chapter 5 because it does not involve the use of overt mathematical models.

REGRESSION REVISITED

Causal regression models work exactly the same way as simple trend line analysis, except that the independent (X) variable represents something other than time. Therefore, trend line analysis is just a specific case of a more general technique. The model is the same one we showed you in chapter 3:

$$(\text{Eqn. 3-3}) \qquad Y = a + bx + e$$

We started with the specific case, trend line analysis, because it is the type of regression model that the working forecaster is most likely to encounter. Most businesses have not yet adopted causal models to any great extent. Also, many forecasting books do not make it clear that trend line analysis, ARMA models, discriminant analysis, and several other methods are just variations on the same theme: regression. We believe that it is easier to master one concept than half a dozen, so we are trying to emphasize their similarities, rather than their differences.

In many regression models of the type discussed in this chapter, a change in the X variable can be thought of as causing a change in the Y variable. For this reason, we often refer to the independent variables in these models as causal variables. A rise in temperature might cause an increase in sales of air conditioners, for example, but the reverse would not be true.

In other models, there isn't any real cause-and-effect relationship, but the model still has predictive value. For example, you could predict the approximate weight of a pumpkin based on its diameter if you wished to do so for some reason. Examination of a large sample of pumpkins would reveal that the weight and diameter are closely associated. Even though neither measurement can be said to "cause" the other, this would still be classified as a causal model.

It is not necessary to say much more about regression here, because it works just about the same way as we explained before. The only difference, again, is that the X variable in a causal model is something other than time. The reader who skipped chapter 3 might want to go back and read about regression before pressing on.

CAUTIONS

Causal models generally are harder to develop than time series models, for obvious reasons. In a typical time series model, the independent variable is already defined for you. There is nothing to identify or measure, aside from recording the dates of transactions, which you would probably do anyway.

In developing a causal model, you need to figure out which factors—such as weather patterns, socioeconomic factors, the value of the Japanese yen, housing starts, the incidence of sunspots, or advertising by competitors—are likely to be good predictors of the dependent variable you are interested in.

Another problem with causal models is that they can be interesting without being useful. Suppose you come up with a really dynamite regression model that explains 85% of the variation in sales for a given product line, based on past data. The causal variables in the model are the price of platinum, barometric pressure, and hog futures. So now what do you do with the model?

Suppose it is February and you need to predict the level of product demand for May. If this were a time series model, you would simply adjust the X variable (or Y_t, or whatever) to reflect a time period three months in the future. But now you have a different situation. Where will hog futures be in May? How do you predict what will happen to platinum, or what the barometric pressure will be?

Someone probably has developed a time series model for each one of these three variables, so you can try making some reasonable projections. But remember that each of those models will have its own error term. Unless you can predict the future values of the *causal* variables with a reasonable degree of accuracy, your model is of little value.

OBTAINING THE DATA

Having identified your causal variables, you must find a way to measure and record their values. This is not always as easy or cheap as you might think. Weather, for example, is a rather localized phenomenon. Anyone who sells anything recognizes the effect of weather. But how does weather exert its effect?

Suppose that your company employs telephone solicitors to sell catalytic ear warmers. Your people might do a better job of selling in warm weather; but the consumers are likely to be more receptive in cold weather. Also, the temperature in your location might be quite different from that in the target consumer area. So where should the data be collected?

And which is more crucial—the daytime high or the nighttime low? Does precipitation figure in? How about wind chill? And what is the date you need to look at? The date when the consumer decides to buy, or when he places the order, or when he receives it? If he returns the item because the weather has changed by the time he gets it, then you haven't achieved much.

In fact, if lead time is crucial, maybe you should forget about forecasting, which sounds like a complicated and expensive proposition anyway. Keeping a high level of stock on hand at all times will ensure that every order is filled promptly. But what about the shelf life of those chemicals? If you overestimate demand for your product, half of them could spoil—or leak, or become denatured, or whatever they do—before you can sell them. Extra storage space costs money, too.

Maybe you could reduce the problem of lead time by advertising the product in September as a Christmas item, with eight weeks allowed for delivery. This takes it out of the category of an impulse item. Then you could just wait until you have received a lot of orders and buy the parts from your distributor all at once. Let *him* worry about developing a causal model.

ADVANTAGES

We are not trying to scare you. We just wanted to let you know why relatively few businesses, particularly small ones, use causal models.

If properly implemented, however, causal models can be highly effective. They are often most useful after demand for a new product has decelerated somewhat. Earlier in the product life cycle, when sales volume is increasing rapidly, time series analysis often works better because causal data are harder to obtain. It's hard to survey a market that is still in the process of defining itself. Also, the newness of a product might be the most powerful factor inducing people to buy, and newness is strictly a function of time.

Another advantage of causal models is that they can be manipulated, at least on paper, to see what kind of future will result. We talked about the scenario approach in chapter 5. What if inflation reaches 9%—how will this affect the number of new building permits issued? What if it reaches 9.5% *and* the summer is dry? What if it reaches 9.75% and it's dry *and* we elect a Republican president?

The most effective judgmental forecasting involves this same type of dialog: people sitting around a conference table, asking "what if" type questions and constructing various future scenarios. By transforming the dialog into a mathematical model, however, you can nail it down. You can reduce the pecking-order effect and the element of subjectivity that creeps into any debate.

Moreover, some causal models can be manipulated in real life and not just on paper. For example, if you are a restaurant manager, you might want to know how the level of salt on your French fries affects soft drink sales, so that you can adjust the salt level accordingly.

You can directly influence things like the amount of salt on French fries. You have less control over things like inflation and weather. But even these differ from time in one important respect: usually you will get a second shot at them, if you wait long enough. Double-digit inflation will be back, sooner or later, so you can test your hypothesis the next time around. Weather patterns also recur. But August 1983 will not return, no matter how many French fries you sold that month.

MULTIPLE REGRESSION

> *The blunt monster with uncounted heads.*
> —William Shakespeare, *King Henry IV*

Until now, when we talked about regression, we meant simple or *univariate* regression. This means regression in which there is only one independent variable, X. As we said, this could be either time or a causal factor.

Most useful causal models, however, contain several independent variables called X_1, X_2, X_3, and so on. Such a model is called a *multivariate* or multiple regression model. If there are three independent variables, for example, the model looks like this:

(Eqn. 7-1) $Y = b_0 + b_1X_1 + b_2X_2 + b_3X_3 + e$

Instead of the Y intercept, represented by the letter a, now you have something in its place called b_0. Formally this is still called the intercept, but it has lost its intuitive meaning. The line is no longer a line but an n-dimensional blob. And instead of one independent variable called X and one slope b, this equation has three different X variables, each one multiplied by its own b. These are no longer called the slope. Instead, they are partial regression coefficients.

You might notice that this looks similar to the AR model, Equation 3-5. The difference is that each X variable in Equation 7-1 represents a whole vector (list) of numbers. In the AR model, each of the values of Y_n just represents one past value of Y.

Multiple regression tends to scare people, both because it involves linear algebra and because you can't draw a very good graph of it. As long as you follow some simple rules, however, multiple regression is not hard to use. As we explained earlier, the problems with this method are mainly practical, rather than mathematical.

True, the math is hard to do with a pencil. The formulas for calculating the b values are more complicated than they were for simple regression. A programmable calculator might not be able to handle the matrix operations because they require too much memory, so you will definitely need a small computer. But nearly every business has one nowadays, and they are not difficult to use. There is no need to write your own program, either. Most of the commercial programs described in chapter 9 will do multiple regression.

The visual part of multiple regression may be harder to deal with than the math. When you had only two variables, X and Y, it was easy to draw a regression line that had an intuitive meaning. But every time you add a variable to the model, you add a dimension to the graph; and since paper is flat, you run out of dimensions very quickly.

With two X variables, you can still represent the relationship with a perspective drawing that looks like a folded or curled sheet of paper. The third axis, on which you plot the second X variable, appears to stick out of the page toward you. This is hard to draw by hand, but great fun with computer graphics. The only problem is interpreting this strange shape once you have drawn it (Fig. 7-1).

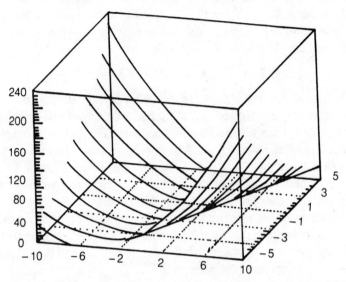

Fig. 7-1. Graph of a Regression Model With Two Independent Variables.

When you get to three or more *X* variables, you can forget about a graph. There is no way to draw it, period. But the same concepts that you learned for simple regression still apply to multiple regression. Instead of a single event, *several* events influence your forecast, just as in real life. That's all.

HOW MANY VARIABLES?

Now visualize a real-life forecasting situation and all the various factors that it might involve. In the ear warmer example, temperature was the only independent variable that we thought we needed, based on the observations of a hypothetical sales force.

We are going to try an exploratory type of problem, in which we will consider several different variables and the ways we might actually use them. The possibilities seem endless at first—but are they?

THINKING THEM UP

To develop a set of reasonable future scenarios to test, use your business intuition and/or a more formal judgmental method such as the jury of executive opinion (chapter 5). In the process, you may well decide that a causal model is not advantageous for your particular business situation.

In chapter 5, we gave you a brief preview of multiple regression in order to illustrate the kinds of mental processes that are likely to go into judgmental forecasting. In that example, we listed some factors that might be expected to influence the length of time that it takes to drive home on the freeway. Such factors might include the density of traffic, the weather, any traffic accidents, road construction work, the time of day, the day of the week, the condition of the tires, and the driver's level of fatigue and/or inebriation.

This seems like an awful lot of variables. As common sense might tell you, it is best not to include too many variables in a multiple regression model. Some of the reasons are as follows:

- If there are a lot of variables, you will need to measure or observe a lot of different things, which can be expensive and time-consuming.

- Your model will not work if it contains a lot of variables but not enough specific data values for each variable. The usual rule is that you need about *seven times* as many observations (data points) as you have variables.

- If some of the X variables are correlated with each other, the model might not be valid. (This problem is called *multicollinearity*.) Therefore, you should be selective about which variables you include.

With these points firmly in mind, let's try to pare down the list of variables in our example. Later on, we can apply some mathematical tests to these variables to determine which ones we should keep. The first step, however, is to think about cause and effect. (Note that this is how we came up with the list in the first place.)

- Intuition tells us that traffic density is crucial to the model, so we would like to keep this one. But how do we collect the data? Subjective impressions of traffic density are not very accurate, and it would be expensive to hire someone to count the cars. Also, *where* do we count them? Should we take the average for the entire stretch of freeway, or the maximum density that occurs anywhere between you and your destination?

- Weather certainly affects how fast people drive and how often they cut in. But is the effect predictable? Rain might make people drive more slowly, but it might also keep them home and thereby reduce traffic density. Hot weather might slow down the traffic by causing accidents and engine overheating, or it might clear the road by encouraging everyone to go to the beach.

And how do you quantify "weather" anyway? Weather is a rather complicated thing. Maybe we can represent it as a *proxy variable*. That is, a single dimension of weather, such as temperature or inches of rainfall, could represent weather.

• Accidents might influence traffic movement more drastically than any other factor. We have all observed how a serious accident can turn a 20-mile stretch of freeway into a parking lot. But the incidence of accidents might be difficult to state in mathematical terms. How nearby must an accident be to qualify? How many lanes must be blocked? Also, the data might be hard to collect, because not all accidents are announced on the radio, or are visible by the time the traffic has cleared. This could get very complicated.

One simple approach to this problem would be to include a variable whose value is 1 if an accident is known to be blocking traffic, or 0 otherwise. (This type of variable, which takes on only the values 1 or 0, often is called a *dummy variable* or yes/no variable.) A few months of data might reveal, for example, that such a blockage increases your average transit time by about 35 minutes.

• Road construction work might affect the model in about the same way that accidents do. It makes the transit time longer. But construction work would have to be a separate variable, because it follows a different pattern. It lasts longer, for example, and it happens less often, and it usually doesn't block the whole freeway.

• The next proposed variable, time of day, clearly influences how long it takes to get home. We feel that we should keep this variable. But does it influence driving speed directly? Or does it instead influence traffic density, which we have already included in the model?

This is a possible case of multicollinearity, in which two of the proposed variables are likely to be closely correlated with each other. Tests are available to determine this. If our suspicion is confirmed, then we must discard one of the two related variables. But which one? Traffic density might seem to be more relevant, because it directly influences your rate of progress. But time of day is easier to measure. All you do is look at your watch.

• The day of the week, like the time of day, might be correlated with traffic density. If so, we can't keep both of those variables. But we said that we might discard traffic density anyway, in favor of the closely related time of day. It is possible that the day of the week will contribute new information that would be lacking with time of day alone, even though both reflect traffic density. We will keep this one and represent it as a *categorical* variable, with values 1, 2, 3, 4, and 5. (We assume that you do not commute on weekends.)

- The condition of the tires was proposed as a variable, because it influences friction as well as the probability of getting a flat. But reliable data will be hard to collect, because flat tires are rare events and we don't know much about the effect of friction. It will not be practical to include this variable, given our present state of knowledge.

- Fatigue definitely affects driving behavior, but how do you measure it accurately? Also, this variable might be strongly correlated with the time of day, and then we would have multicollinearity again. We will have to discard it.

- Alcohol is like weather, in that it influences driving behavior in somewhat unpredictable ways. You might go faster or slower. You might be killed, in which case you would lose all interest in developing a regression model. Also, unless drunkenness is your habitual state, it will be hard to collect enough data to use in the model. We will discard this variable.

Well, we have only five variables left: weather, time of day, day of the week, accidents, and road construction. And we are not at all confident that the day of the week will be relevant, or that weather will tell us much, or that accidents can be quantified in a satisfactory manner.

Developing a multiple regression model typically proceeds in this fashion. You start out thinking that the problem is so complex that it will require an unwieldy number of variables. Dozens, even hundreds, come to mind. It's like the Hydra in Greek mythology: you dispose of one head and nine more seem to grow in its place. But as you deal with them systematically, the variables begin to go away. You might wind up without any.

CHECKING THE MODEL

In general, a linear multiple regression model needs to satisfy the following criteria. We talked about some of these before, but they bear repetition. If you are not a statistician, you might need to hire one to check your conclusions:

- There must be a linear relationship between the independent variables X_1, X_2, . . . and the dependent variable Y. If the relationship is not linear, often you can fix this by transforming the variables (for example, by taking the logarithm).

- The values of the dependent variable Y must be independent of one another. If they are not, you have autocorrelation, which was discussed earlier in connection with time series models. This is less often a problem in causal models, but you can check the possibility by using the Durbin-Watson test. It is included in most major statistical packages.

- The independent variables X_1, X_2, ... must be independent of one another. If they are not, you have multicollinearity. You detect this by checking what is called the correlation matrix (a table of correlation coefficients, r, between all combinations of the X and Y variables). Most statistical programs do this. You correct the problem by throwing out or transforming some of the X variables.

- The number of observations must exceed the number of independent variables. Again, a common rule is that you must have at least seven times as many data values as independent variables.

- The variance of the error term in the model must be constant. This condition is called *homoscedasticity*. If it is violated, this is not a crime in most states, but then you have *heteroscedasticity*. Two statistical procedures called Bartlett's test and the Goldfeld-Quandt test can be used to check this possibility. Some statistical programs do these tests.

KEEPING TIME

Not all the independent variables in a multiple regression model need to be causal variables. You can also throw in time as one of the X variables. The values of this variable would be 1, 2, 3, etc., just as in simple trend line analysis. This type of combined model is very commonly used, despite the risk of misleading results due to autocorrelation.

STEPWISE MULTIPLE REGRESSION

The stepwise method is one popular way to do a multiple regression problem on the computer. Many statistical software packages, including some public domain programs, include this as an option.

When you have several independent (X) variables and you are not sure which ones are the most useful for forecasting, you might want to perform the regression calculations in a stepwise fashion. What this means is that the computer will add the variables into the model one at a time, starting with the one that it determines to have the most explanatory value.

In other words, the first part of the computer printout will show the results of the regression calculations as if there were only one X variable in the model. The X that appears there will be the one that does the best job of predicting Y. Then the printout will show the results of the calculations using that same X variable *plus* a second one. It will show how much more of the variation in the data has been explained by adding this second variable. It will continue in this manner until all the variables have been included.

Some authors, however, recommend that stepwise regression be used with caution or even avoided because of potentially misleading results. See reference 1 for a discussion.

Backward stepwise elimination is the reverse of stepwise multiple regression. The procedure starts with all the variables in the model and eliminates them one at a time.

TWO-STAGE FORECASTING

In chapter 6, we demonstrated several different ways to calculate a forecast using exponential smoothing. We should explain that ES is not always an end in itself. Sometimes it is used as an intermediate step in a more complex forecasting process that involves causal variables. For example, ES can be used for smoothing time series data before it is subjected to a least squares regression analysis.

In one study, a two-stage analysis of this kind was used in calculating short-term forecasts for sales and production of eight synthetic organic chemicals.[2] First, the time series data values were smoothed through double exponential smoothing. This step reduced the amount of noise in the series. Then the resulting smoothed values were used in a stepwise multiple regression model with six independent variables. Five of these predictors were standard economic indices related to the organic chemical market. In addition, the model included time as a sixth independent variable.

The results were good, in the sense that the regression models had high R values. (Much of the random error had already been polished away by the smoothing step.) Also, the majority of actual data values for the next forecast interval fell within a 99% confidence interval around the forecasts.

Extra Credit Problem: Does the last sentence of the previous paragraph mean that the forecasts were 99% accurate?

DISCRIMINANT ANALYSIS

This method is very similar to multiple regression, except that the outcome variable stands for an attribute rather than a continuous measurement. The outcome variable can take on two or more values, depending on what you want to predict. If it has only two possible values, 0 or 1, then this is sometimes called a *probit regression* (or a logistic regression, depending upon the distribution that is used).

For example, you might want to predict whether or not certain business customers will pay their bills. By looking at your past records on other customers, you have previously determined that five characteristics, taken as a group, tend to discriminate good accounts from deadbeats. Some of these characteristics might be their number of years in business, size of the loan, Dun and Bradstreet rating, and so on.

You could set up a discriminant function with five X variables, representing those five characteristics, and use it to assess new customers that come along. The value of the discriminant function, as it is called, would determine group membership: Group 1, those that pay, and Group 2, those that don't. You could use this information when deciding whether to give a prompt payment discount, for example, or whether to extend a line of credit.

Or you might want to predict which customers will tend to switch brands at least once a year and which will tend to stay with the same product. (We talked about this in chapter 5 in the section on Markov chains.) Again, you would start by finding some characteristics that tend to distinguish the two groups: those that switch and those that don't.

In both cases, the Y variable would take on either of two values, 1 or 0. These values would correspond to the two groups that you are interested in: payers and deadbeats, switchers and nonswitchers. In other words, this is very much like multiple regression. But instead of using the model to predict a numeric value, such as how many widgets they will buy, you are using it to make a yes-no type of decision about them.

CANONICAL CORRELATION

This method is something like multiple regression, except that you predict a whole set of dependent variables at once. If you want to try it, use one of the statistical software packages that include it, such as STATGRAPHICS or BMDP.

We have always hated canonical correlation, so we were hoping to omit it from this book. A long time ago, we read a paper that used this method to prove something regarding frogs. But it doesn't seem to be used very much in business forecasting and we were happy to learn that Armstrong does not care for it either.[3]

ECONOMETRIC MODELS

Econometric modeling is the process of forecasting changes in the national or world economy on the basis of a mathematical model. Usually this incorporates judgmental forecasting methods (chapter 5) as well as multiple regression analysis.

This level of forecasting is also called *macro* forecasting, to indicate that it deals with events on a large scale. *Micro* forecasting, by contrast, is the level practiced by most businesses when predicting material requirements, product demand, and so on. Multiple regression and other complex causal models seem to be used primarily at the macro level. Our book is mainly about micro forecasting principles, so we will not dwell on this topic.

MARMA MODELS

Man is a creature who lives not upon bread alone but principally by catch-words.
　　　　　　　　　　　　　—Robert Louis Stevenson

We have shown that it is possible, even commonplace, to include time as an independent variable in a regression model. If time is the only independent variable, the result is called trend line analysis. If there are other independent variables as well, the model has no special name. It is just a multiple regression model with time thrown in.

As we explained, ARMA models were developed in response to some of the shortcomings of trend line analysis. Causal models, on the other hand, can provide more information than time series analysis alone. It would be nice to be able to combine the virtues of both types of model, and methods are being developed for doing just that. From the viewpoint of the average business forecaster, however, these methods are still largely on the drawing board.[4]

The term MARMA stands for "multivariate ARMA," which means a combined time series and causal regression model. The complexity of such a model depends on how the variables in the model influence one another. Some of these models involve sets of simultaneous equations and are so hairy that we will not try to deal with them here.

In the simplest case, however, the model can be written as a single equation, just like the other models we have shown you. A MARMA model of this type is sometimes called a *transfer function* model. For example:

$$\text{(Eqn. 7-2)} \quad Y_t = b_0 + b_1 Y_{t-1} + b_2 X_{1.t} + b_3 X_{2.t} + e$$

You might think of this as a first-order AR model that also includes two causal variables, X_1 and X_2. The notation Y_t means "the value of Y at time t," just as it did in the standard AR model. Similarly, Y_{t-1} means "the value of Y in the time period previous to time t."

The b values are coefficients, just as they were in the other models. The notation $X_{1.t}$ means "the value of variable X_1 at time t" and $X_{2.t}$ means "the value of variable X_2 at time t." The letter e represents the error term as usual.

Of all mathematical forecasting techniques, MARMA models seem the most promising in many respects. They take up where ARMA leaves off, by considering the effects of causal factors in addition to the patterns shown by past data. Their major drawback, however, is their mathematical complexity.

Of the microcomputer software we have reviewed (chapter 9), only FORECAST PRO offers even a simple MARMA-type model. They call it "dynamic regression," and it consists of a single-equation model without the MA term. (Using our acronyms, it would be a MAR model.) We are told that the University of Wisconsin Department of Statistics also has a multiple time series program called WMTS. We do not know whether it is generally available or not.

Here is a hypothetical example of a situation where a simple MARMA model might be useful. (The type of MARMA model implied by this example is called an *intervention model*.)

Imagine that your company manufactures small iodine tablets that are used to purify drinking water. They have a limited shelf life, so you can't make too many in advance. Your chief customers are stores and mail-order houses that sell camping equipment. Sales have been edging upward for the past five years, with a seasonal peak in demand at the beginning of every summer and some other fluctuations that seem to be random. You use a SARIMA time series model for forecasting demand, and it performs satisfactorily.

All of a sudden, two years ago, your orders quadrupled for about two weeks. It was not summer, and you were wholly unprepared. Your faithful staff worked like mad, making little pills around the clock, but many orders were delayed and you might have lost some customers.

Luckily, however, you did not fire your statistician, who gave you a clue by pointing out that most of the unexpected orders originated in southern California. You started calling some of the dealers and asking them why the iodine pills were moving so briskly. They explained that the Caltech scientists had been at it again, predicting a big California earthquake. The local survivalists felt that the sequelae of a large earthquake might include a polluted water supply; so they began stocking up on your tablets.

You advised your statistician to watch the wire service reports carefully from then on, and a pattern emerged. The two of you concluded that, whenever there is a big earthquake scare, your orders are likely to increase a week or two later, remain up for about a week, and then taper off. Now you have a factor to include in a causal model.

But you don't want to stop using time series analysis either, because it works so well most of the time. One simple solution would be to institute a rule of thumb: In times of earthquake mania, ignore the computer-generated time series forecast and make four times as many pills. (In practice, this is comparable to what many businesses do.)

Or you could automate the process instead, by adding a dummy variable (quake/no quake) to the model to do the same thing: If quake, multiply by four; if no quake, use only the time series portion of the model. At this point, you would have a simple intervention model, more or less. This is a type of MARMA model. (But since this one is seasonal and trending, maybe you would call it SMARIMA. Names of time series models always sound like the names of monsters in Japanese movies.)

And you can keep going. For example, the model could be refined so that it evaluates the significance of the earthquake, instead of rating them all alike. A small tremor in outer Mongolia is less likely to alarm Americans than a quake that kills 20,000 people in Peru. And the latter, unfortunately, will not impress us as much as a jiggle that cracks our own concrete retaining wall in Tarzana. Therefore, you might want to classify news reports according to their expected impact on your sales.

Your statistician could go on gleefully refining your MARMA model forever, in fact, to account for all sorts of variables. But it might turn out that it requires a month of his effort to refine the model enough to sell five more bottles of pills. Statisticians this smart rarely work cheap, and you would have to decide at what point the process ceased to be cost-effective.

The preceding example should suggest some reasons why MARMA is not used by most businesses, nor given more than a passing mention in most forecasting books:

- MARMA is a highly complex method, and a company without a statistician would have a hard time using it. Improved software might eventually remove this difficulty.

- Many businesses have found that introducing a complex forecasting system results in only a slight increase in forecasting accuracy. The potential benefit of such a model might not offset the initial costs and confusion.

- Few companies are using MARMA models at present, so other companies have little opportunity to see whether it works or not. Until its effectiveness becomes widely known, businesses are unwilling to risk using it. Conversely, until more companies start using it, its effectiveness will not become widely known.

References 5 and 6 provide additional information regarding MARMA models.

SUMMARY

Causal regression models use the same mathematical procedures as trend line analysis. The difference is that the independent variables in causal models represent something other than time. Multiple regression models are those that include two or more independent variables. This method often is used in econometric modeling. Discriminant analysis is a form of multiple regression used to classify groups. MARMA models combine the features of ARMA time series and causal models.

REVIEW QUESTIONS

1. Pick a product line with which you are familiar, and list some factors that are likely to influence sales. Then explain which of these factors you might include in a multiple regression model, and why.

2. Do you think most businesses could benefit from causal forecasting? Explain your answer.

3. Is astrology an example of causal forecasting, judgmental forecasting, or neither? Explain your answer.

4. Is a MARMA model the same as a multiple regression model that includes time as one independent variable?

ENDNOTES

1. B. Chalmer, *Understanding Statistics* (New York: Marcel Dekker, Inc., 1987).

2. B. S. Baxter, "Forecasting Sales and Production of Synthetic Organic Chemicals With Microcomputers." M.S. Thesis, University of Arkansas, (1987).

3. J. S. Armstrong, *Long-Range Forecasting: From Crystal Ball to Computer* (New York: John Wiley & Sons, 1985), 225.

4. P. Newbold, "Time-Series Model Building and Forecasting: A Survey," in *Forecasting: Studies in the Management Sciences*, Volume 12, edited by S. Makridakis and S. C. Wheelwright, (Amsterdam: North-Holland Publishing Company, 1979), 59-74.

5. G. M. Jenkins, and A. S. Alavi, "Some Aspects of Modelling and Forecasting Multivariate Time Series," *Journal of Time Series Analysis* 2(1981):1-47.

6. L. M. Terry, and W. R. Terry, "A Multiple Time Series Analysis of Cotton-Polyester Market Competition," in "Applied Time Series Analysis," proceedings of the International Conference Held at Houston, Texas, August 1981, edited by O. D. Anderson and M. R. Perryman (Amsterdam: North-Holland Publishing Company, 1982), 409-413.

8
Forecast Monitoring and Revision

Sentence first—verdict afterwards.

—Lewis Carroll

This chapter will introduce you to the following topics:

- How to tell whether a forecasting model is working.
- How to take corrective action if it is not.

CRITERIA

Forecasting is like shooting arrows at a target that is a long way off, on a windy day. You won't hit the bull's-eye very often, but you shouldn't miss the whole bale of hay, either.

This is why we explained confidence intervals back in chapter 3. A confidence interval is like one of the circles on the target. Your goal is to have the arrow land somewhere inside this circle most of the time. If it is very windy, or if the target is very far away, then you might have to be satisfied with one of the outermost circles. (You might also have to accept losing a few arrows.)

It is up to management to decide what level of accuracy is acceptable, but it is up to the forecaster to decide how accurate the forecast *can* be. Management should not require forecasts to be accurate within 1 or 5 percent, if the data varies so much that this level of accuracy is impossible. A point estimate will rarely be accurate. An interval forecast should be accurate—if you make the interval wide enough.

WHEN TO TEST

Testing a forecasting model requires some ingenuity. The most obvious way to do it is to wait and see how well the model predicts the future. But by the time the future arrives, it is too late to change the model for that forecast interval, and your company might have lost some money.

Ideally, you should have some idea of how well the model works even before you start using it. Later, as new data start to come in, you should compare them with the forecast values and see if any fine tuning is required. Therefore, there are at least two stages in the forecasting process at which the accuracy of a model should be checked: (1) at the time the new model is developed, and (2) periodically thereafter.

A good forecast model can have various levels of goodness. This sounds like a funny word, but it is one that statisticians use all the time. You may have heard the expression "goodness of fit," which means how well the forecasting model fits, or reproduces, the data that are already known.

TESTING A NEW MODEL

In the development stage, one quick way to check a variable in a causal model is to use the correlation coefficient. As we explained in chapter 6, this test shows how closely the variables in a model are associated with each other, so you can see if you are on the right track.

For example, if rain is a variable that figures prominently in your new model of umbrella sales, at some point you might want to gather some old data on meteorological conditions and sales volume and then calculate r. If the two variables aren't associated after all, then you need to start over.

You can also test a regression model by using analysis of variance, or ANOVA, which we talked about in chapter 3. ANOVA will tell you whether the regression model is doing a good job of explaining the existing data. Almost every statistical software package will do this test for you. There is no need to do tedious calculations by hand.

Some forecasting programs, such as FORECAST PRO (chapter 9), create an audit trail which compares various forecasting models to see which one does the best job of fitting the past data. This feature enables you to select the model that is likely to work best before you start to use it.

In the early stages of development, it's also a good idea to have a statistician look at your model (even if you are a statistician yourself). A model might fit the available data perfectly and still be a bad model, if you have unwittingly violated one or more of the requirements for the procedure.

For example, suppose that you have only five data values, one for each month that you have been selling copper-plated freens. At this stage, all you can really use is judgment, perhaps in combination with one of the simplest time series models such as moving averages. So if you are about to launch a model with twenty-seven independent variables, which you believe will account for every possible reason why people might buy a freen, then you are in trouble. It doesn't matter whether it fits those five data values or not. It simply won't work for future values.

It won't work—but if this is the way you tell your computer to set up the model, it will comply. Five data points—great! Twenty-seven variables—why not? Unless you are using a fairly sophisticated expert system, it won't say a word. It will graciously give you all the rope you need to hang yourself.

Chapter 7 lists the criteria that must be met in order for a causal model to be valid. You should review these assumptions at this point and be certain that they are met.

EXPLOITING THE NAIVE MODEL

If this heading sounds naughty, shame on you. A *naive model* is just a rule which states that the forecast for the next interval is the same as the observed value for the most recent interval. In other words, it assumes that nothing will change.

This model—which is also called NF1 (naive forecast 1), last period forecasting, or the random walk model—was mentioned previously in chapter 6. We promised that it would turn out to have some value, other than predicting the stock market, and now we are about to make good.

The naive model provides a very simple test of the effectiveness of your forecasting model. This is called the naive model test, and it has been used since the 1940s.[1] At the beginning of each forecast interval (month or whatever), you make two forecasts, one using your hopeful new model and the other using the naive model. After you have done this a number of times, you compare the two sets of figures to see whether one model did a better job than the other.

But how do we define a "better job"? Many forecasters have proposed that the accuracy of a model should be judged by the percentage of total *change* that the model predicts.[1] Suppose, for example, that you have been using the naive model test for some time when evaluating forecasts for your various product lines. You have found that the average forecast error for the naive model is 10%. In other words, the naive model produces forecasts that are, on the average, about 10% higher or lower than actual sales.

Suppose, also, that your usual forecasting procedure is exponential smoothing. For your particular business situation, you have found that this method yields an average forecast error of 7%. This means the ES method passes the naive model test.

From another viewpoint, however, the ES model still isn't doing a spectacular job. Think of it this way: You can predict sales to within 10% without doing any calculations at all, just by assuming that nothing will change. Using ES, you can predict sales to within 7%—an improvement of only 3 percentage points. Therefore, the ES model is explaining only 30% of the total change in sales ($^3/_{10} = 0.30$).

But let's stick with the ES model for the time being. Your present objective is to compare it with the naive model for a relatively new product. A forecasting method can be effective for some products but not for others, so you need to check. Let's say the product has been out for a year. (You need to accumulate about 12 intervals of data before you can really start forecasting. In the meantime, of course, you have been making some educated guesses.)

Last month, your sales for this new product totaled $1000. The naive model predicts that next month's sales also will be $1000, plus or minus 10% in this case. Thus the NF1 interval forecast could be stated as $900 to $1100. (This is an "interval" in the informal sense. It doesn't refer to a specific probability level.)

When you plug the past year's data into the ES model, it happens in this case that you come up with a forecast of $1800. But when the actual figures come in, you find that sales for the month total $1200. In this case, the naive model seems to have won. It was off by 20%, but it was still closer to the target than the ES model, which was in error by 50%.

Don't throw out the ES model just yet. It is possible, of course, that the pattern of demand for this product is different and that you need a random walk model. But maybe there is a seasonal pattern that you couldn't detect with only a year of data, so you need a seasonal model. Or perhaps there was a dip in sales this month because of random factors that no model could predict. Before making a decision, you need to continue running both forecasts for a reasonable number of months.

Many forecasting programs include a statistical test called Theil's U coefficient, which can be used for evaluating the accuracy of a forecast. The more common version of this test compares the forecast value with the value obtained using a random walk model.[2] You can't run the test on a single forecast; you need a series of them.

While you are accumulating the required series of data values for more testing, time and profits are evaporating. Thus you might want to start testing a couple of other forecasting methods alongside these two. If you are using a computer, this will take only a few extra seconds each month.

AIC AND BIC

These are two effective tests that are often used to select the best forecasting model from among several candidates. AIC, developed by a statistician named Akaike, stands for "Akaike Information Criterion." BIC is a variation on this method.[3]

The relative virtues of the two tests have been the subject of much debate, which we do not propose to summarize here. These are the methods that the program FORECAST PRO uses to select a forecasting model, if you exercise the audit trail option.

TESTING A WORKING MODEL

Once you are satisfied that you have gotten the major bugs out of your new forecasting model, naturally you will want to move past the developmental stage. You want to start using the model and basing some real decisions on it. But it is important to remain open-minded at this stage and avoid the temptation to defend your brainchild too vigorously. This is the way businesses sometimes get stuck with inadequate forecasting methods.

Several different tests are available for monitoring the performance of a working model. Two of the simplest and most common tests are called the *filter* and the *tracking signal*. Many of the forecasting programs for mainframe computers offer one or both of these tests as options. For some reason, however, the microcomputer programs that we have reviewed do not include either of these tests. In any case, you can do these tests on paper fairly easily, or you can write your own short program to do them.

FILTER

The name of this method should not be confused with adaptive filtering (chapter 6). The filter—generally called a demand filter or sales filter, depending on what you are forecasting—is a test that looks at each forecast to see how different it is from the actual data value, once the latter is known.

If the forecast is wrong by more than a certain amount, the result is called a *filter trip* (because it's similar to tripping an alarm). Then the program notifies you that the forecast is outside the limits you have set. Usually these limits are pretty generous.

With most forecasting systems, the user decides what confidence level to use for the filter. You might start, for example, by setting the limits for the filter at 4 times the value of MAD. At this setting, the filter is not "tripped" unless the forecast falls outside a 99.8% confidence interval around the actual value.

These are very wide limits. The forecast would have to be a long way off in order to be flagged as an error. (Back in chapter 3, we said that confidence limits for most things are set at 95%, but that was in a different type of situation. Here, we want to give the forecasting system the benefit of the doubt, because no one wants to have to deal with a lot of filter trips.)

Say the March forecast for widget demand is 103. The actual demand for widgets in March turns out to be 220. We can see right away that the forecast was wrong. The purpose of the demand filter is to tell us whether the forecast was wrong enough to make us question the validity of the model we are using.

In this example, the value of MAD that we have calculated, based on (say) two years of demand history, is 10. So the highest forecast that the demand filter will accept is:

$$220 + (4)(10) = 260$$

and the lowest forecast that the demand filter will accept is:

$$220 - (4)(10) = 180$$

The forecast, 103, is not just wrong, it is *very* wrong. It is way below the lower limit of 180, so it is appropriate that the system should flag it as an error.

In a situation like this, the forecaster needs to go back and see what went wrong. It may be necessary to reinitialize the system, using a different set of values or assumptions. Perhaps the pattern of demand has changed, or possibly the item was classified incorrectly in the first place. Or maybe it was a one-time event and there isn't anything you can do about it.

TRACKING SIGNAL

Many mainframe forecasting programs also include a routine called the tracking signal. Instead of testing each individual forecast, the way the filter does, the tracking signal monitors all the recent forecasts as a group, to see if they are wrong in some consistent way.

When we compared forecasting to archery, you might recall that we mentioned wind. Product demand is influenced by many random events that tend to throw the forecast off. Wind tends to deflect arrows in much the same way.

But what if the wind blows consistently in one direction for a while, so that the arrows always land too far to the right? If you are aware of that fact, you can correct for it. This is what the tracking signal enables you to do.

For example, the tracking signal might show that the forecasts tend to be too low every month. You would want to adjust the system to prevent this from happening. Maybe there is an upward trend in product demand which you are not aware of, or possibly you have a math error somewhere.

Two common methods for calculating the tracking signal are the *sum of errors* (or *cusum*, for cumulative sum) and the *smoothed error*. "Error" means the difference (positive or negative) between the forecast and the actual data value for any given month. "Smoothed" just means that we use the exponentially smoothed average of past errors.

Incidentally, when we refer to this type of error, we don't necessarily mean that the forecaster has screwed up. Error is inevitable in statistics. Even if you always use the right method, it will not always work. The sad thing about statistics is that you *know* you will be wrong some of the time. If you are a well-adjusted person, probably you know this anyway. But at least you don't know how often it will happen, so you can tell yourself that it is a very rare event. In statistics, you know exactly how often you will be wrong. You just don't know when.

If you determine that your forecast is reliable at the 95% confidence level, for example, this sounds good. But remember what else you are saying: It is 5% likely to be *wrong*. And 5% of the time, by golly, it *will* be wrong.

But enough philosophy. Let's get back to the tracking signal. You are trying to keep track of the average forecast error, so that you can compare it with some standard measure of dispersion (see chapter 3).

SUM OF ERRORS METHOD

There are several different kinds of cusums. The simple cusum, for example, just adds up all the error terms and divides by the smoothed MAD.[4] In other words, at the end of each forecast interval you add the latest forecast error to a running total of all the errors. Then you update the value of MAD by simple exponential smoothing. Finally, you get the ratio of the two. This ratio is the tracking signal.

The tracking signal should be low, if everything is going well, because the sum of the forecast errors should be close to zero. In other words, if the forecast is too high about as often as it is too low, half of the errors will be positive numbers and the other half will be negative, and they should cancel each other out. Therefore, a high tracking signal indicates a problem.

To test the tracking signal, you see if it exceeds a critical value C. You set the value of C according to the confidence level that you want, as shown in the following table:

Confidence Level	C = 0.1	= 0.2	= 0.3
0.20	3.6	2.6	2.1
0.10	4.7	2.9	2.8
0.05	5.6	4.1	3.5
0.04	5.9	4.3	3.7
0.03	6.3	4.6	3.9
0.02	6.8	5.0	4.3
0.01	7.5	5.6	4.9

SMOOTHED ERROR METHOD

This is the same as the previous method, except that the top part of the ratio is the smoothed error instead of the sum of all the errors. To update the smoothed error for the current month, a typical program does the following:

New Smoothed Error =
(a) × (Current Deviation) + (1-*a*) × (Old Smoothed Error)

where a is some reasonable value that you selected earlier.

The tracking signal would be the absolute value of this new smoothed error, divided by the MAD:

$$\text{Tracking Signal} = \frac{|\text{Smoothed Error}|}{\text{MAD}}$$

The tracking signal is always less than 1.0, because the absolute value of the smoothed error always is less than MAD. You can see why if you think about where these numbers came from.

As we said, if the model is working, the smoothed error should stay near zero. But if there are more errors in one direction than the other, then the smoothed error will be larger, and this will make the tracking signal larger.

The user decides how many random trips the system should allow to occur. In other words, sometimes the tracking signal will be tripped just because of random fluctuations, not because there is a consistent error in the forecasts. You must decide what percentage of the time you are willing to have this happen. Of course, you might like to specify zero. But if you set the level that low, a lot of genuine errors also are going to slip through the net.

According to one study, the smoothed-error tracking signal is recommended if the smoothing constant is 0.1. For higher values of alpha, however, the simple cusum tracking signal gives better results.[5]

THE LINE OF PERFECT FORECASTS

There are several different graphic devices that you can use for monitoring forecasts. Many people find a graph more informative than a list of numbers.

For example, suppose that your forecasts are always 100% perfect. The forecast for each month turns out to be the same as actual sales for that month. If you draw a graph with the forecasts on one axis and the actual sales on the other, then the points should form a straight line at a 45-degree angle to the coordinate system, like the straight line shown in Fig. 8-1.

In real life, your forecasts will not be perfect. But the degree to which the actual graph resembles this ''ideal'' graph can be used as a rough indicator of how well you are doing. As shown in Fig. 8-1, the line of perfect forecasts divides the coordinate system into six areas. On top of this diagram, you plot your actual forecasts in the form of a

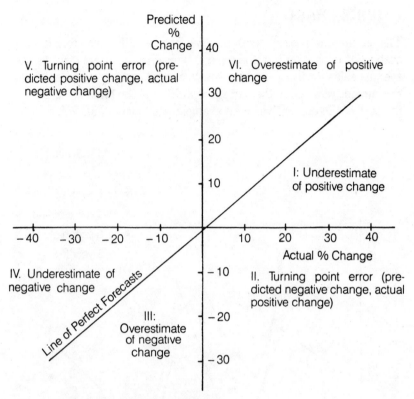

Fig. 8-1. Prediction-Realization Diagram.

scatter graph. The areas where the points fall indicate the magnitude of the various sources of forecast error:

- Points falling in the sections labelled II and V indicate errors in predicting *turning points*. In other words, these points represent times when the forecaster expected an upward trend but got a downward one, and vice versa.

- Points falling in sections I and VI result when the forecaster correctly predicted an upward trend, but the forecast value was in error (or outside the acceptable interval).

- Points falling in sections III and IV result when the forecaster correctly predicted a downward trend, but the forecast value was in error (or outside the acceptable interval).

A graph of this type is often called a *prediction-realization diagram*.

LADDER CHART

This is another type of chart that is often used for monitoring forecasts. For each month of the year, a typical ladder chart displays the average sales for five years, the five-year high and low value, sales for the current year (up to the current month), and the forecast values for the rest of the current year. An example is shown in Fig. 8-2.

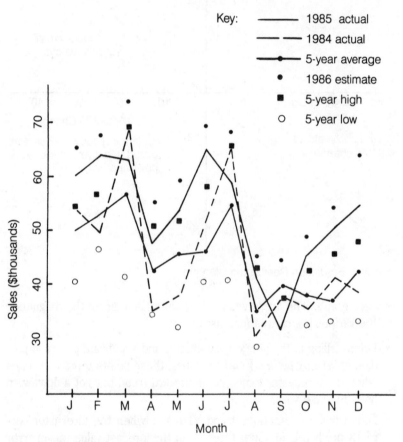

Fig. 8-2. Sample Ladder Chart.

The purpose of the five-year average line is to indicate the seasonal pattern. This method can be viewed as either an alternative or an adjunct to mathematical methods for detecting a seasonal pattern. The line for the current year, including the forecast values, can be compared visually with the other lines to see if it appears to be reasonable.

CONTROL CHART

This type of chart should be familiar to engineers and other people involved in quality control work. Some product or process is measured periodically to see whether it falls within required limits, and the result is plotted on a graph. Quality control standards and procedures should be applied to everything that your company makes, including forecasts.

In chapter 3, we talked about confidence intervals and how you construct them. An interval forecast, as you perhaps recall, is a range of values that represents the forecast flanked by its upper and lower confidence limit. It looks something like this:

$$\overline{X} \pm 2s$$

where $\overline{X}$ is the forecast value and s is the standard deviation. In this example, the confidence level is set at about 95%, because an interval of two standard deviations works out to about that level. If the actual value falls outside the limits of this interval forecast, then there is only about a 5% chance that the forecasting model is on target.

This is basically what we did with the filter method discussed earlier in the chapter. We checked each individual forecast, as well as all the forecasts collectively, to see whether they were straying outside a defined confidence interval. The only difference was that we used MAD instead of the standard deviation in those examples. A control chart is a way of representing this same procedure on paper. An example of a control chart is shown in Fig. 8-3.

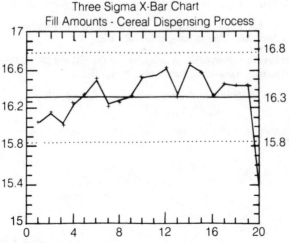

Three Sigma X-Bar Chart
Fill Amounts - Cereal Dispensing Process

Fig. 8-3. Sample Control Chart.

SUMMARY

A forecasting model must be checked periodically, both during the development stage and after the model is in use. Some of the most common testing methods include the correlation coefficient, ANOVA, the AIC and BIC tests, the naive model test, the filter, and the tracking signal. Graphic devices for monitoring forecast performance include prediction-realization diagrams, ladder charts, and control charts.

REVIEW QUESTIONS

1. Why is it important to monitor a forecasting system?

2. At what stage in the forecast model development process do you stop testing your model?

3. Would you buy a forecasting program that did not include a built-in forecast monitoring function?

ENDNOTES

1. R. L. McLaughlin, "Forecasting Models: Sophisticated or Naive?" *Journal of Forecasting* 2(1983):274-276.

2. B. Steece, "Evaluation of Forecasts," in *The Handbook of Forecasting: A Manager's Guide*, (New York: John Wiley & Sons, 1982), 457-468.

3. A. B. Koehler, E. S. Murphree, "A comparison of the AIC and BIC on Empirical Data," Sixth International Symposium on Forecasting, Paris (1986).

4. R. G. Brown, *Statistical Forecasting for Inventory Control*. (New York: McGraw-Hill, 1959).

5. E. S. Gardner, Jr. "Automatic Monitoring of Forecast Errors," *Journal of Forecasting* 2(1983):1-21.

9
Computers and Forecasting

You can pull the computer's plug, but you can't pull its leg.

—Daniel S. Compton

This chapter will introduce you to the following topics:

- The reasons why computer access and computer literacy are essential to the modern forecaster.
- A brief review of some forecasting programs that are currently available for microcomputers.
- Fixing a computer.

You can be a good forecaster even if you hate mathematics. If you also hate computers, however, you might consider another line of work.

In this chapter, we are assuming that your company already has a microcomputer or a few hundred dollars to invest in one. Now you have to buy a forecasting program—and tell it what you want it to do. This last point is crucial because without proper guidance the thing will run amok.

In the first eight chapters, we explained how the various forecasting methods work, so that you could hold an intelligent dialog with your computer (and possibly with your boss). The rest is fairly easy.

WHY A COMPUTER?

Doing routine, repetitive calculations by hand is unbelievably boring and time-consuming. It also invites error, and this is a field in which error can be expensive. Computers are cheap, and most offices nowadays already have them. Forecasting programs are available in stores, so you don't need to know anything about programming. Most of these programs are relatively inexpensive. In fact, some of them are free.

THINK SMALL

We have a client who pays $50,000 per year for a site license for a major statistical software package. But he uses the program to generate a few means and standard deviations that could be done faster on a $5 hand calculator.

We have another client who bought an IBM mainframe computer and a $500,000 integrated software package that is supposed to do forecasting and inventory control. The system is used to print a few graphs which no one in the organization uses for anything.

We have a client—well, you get the general idea.

More is not necessarily better. If you have reason to believe that sinking a million bucks into a forecasting system will demoralize your competition or impress your clients, then go ahead and do it. But if you don't have the million, don't be discouraged. Between $5 and $500 worth of software will get you almost every forecasting method covered in our book.

You will also need a PC to run it on. Probably you have one or more of these in your office already. If not, consider a generic or "no-name" computer. Many of these are just as good as the name brands—as long as you understand how they work, because the directions might be in Chinese.

The next step toward economy is to buy a used computer. This is not nearly as risky as buying a used car, because there is a lot less to break down, and anyway you don't entrust your life to the thing. It won't blow up in your face. Local computer newsletters and tabloids are published in most large cities, and their classified ads are a veritable gold mine of used computer equipment. These newsletters usually are available for free in computer stores.

FORECASTING SOFTWARE

Until a few years ago, good statistical software was hard to find. Recently, however, forecasting and general-purpose statistical programs have been multiplying at an alarming rate. A 1985 review article in the *Journal of Forecasting* listed more than 90 such programs.[1] By 1986, hundreds of statistics programs were available for the IBM PC alone.[2] A full range of statistical software also is available for larger computers.[3,4]

Almost any general statistical software package can be used for business forecasting, but some of them are more convenient for this purpose than others. Before selecting a program, you need to decide which forecasting techniques you want to use, how much money you want to spend, how much time you can spend learning to use the program, and how you want the output to look.

All stats packages do least squares regression, for example, but only a few of them offer adaptive filtering or multivariate time series models. Some of the programs have beautiful color graphics—but if you don't have a color plotter, all you can do with the graphics is admire them on the screen. A few of the graphics programs won't talk to a plotter even if you have one.

Some programs assume that you are a mathematician and ask you a lot of questions; others do the whole job for you. And some are oriented toward a particular type of forecasting, such as econometric modeling, judgmental forecasting based on financial scenarios, or classical time series analysis.

In this chapter, we will review thirteen programs that can be used for forecasting on the IBM PC or compatibles. Many of these programs also are available in versions for other computers. We could not possibly review everything on the market, but we tried to anticipate the needs of as many readers as possible. A book published in 1986 describes several other statistical programs for the PC, but the reviews already have become somewhat outdated; publishers revise their software so often that it's impossible to keep up.[5]

The following organization, called SMUG, is a valuable source of information about forecasting software:

STATISTICIAN'S MICROCOMPUTER USER'S GROUP
Paul Marsh, Editor
Department of Statistics
Box 8203
North Carolina State University
Raleigh, NC 27695-8203

Usually it's a good idea to check some recent computer magazines or talk to some other business users when you are deciding on a forecasting program. Many publishers will send you a demo disk for a small fee, but remember that these are carefully designed to show the program at its best. You don't get the bad news until you buy the whole thing.

Some of the best-known statistical packages have already been so extensively reviewed, advertised, and debated elsewhere that we decided to skip them. Examples are BMDP, SPSS, and SAS. BMDP, for example, has been around since 1961. It has been thoroughly tested over the years, product support is excellent, and the manual is the size of a small encyclopedia, but not everyone likes the program or can afford it. The publisher is BMDP Statistical Software in Los Angeles.

Table 9-1 on pages 144 and 145, lists the various forecasting methods discussed in our book and tells which of the reviewed programs included them as of early 1989. The table also includes BMDP, because we have used it for fifteen years and are highly familiar with it.

We will now address the delicate subject of cost. These programs range in price from under $35 to over $1500. This may not sound like a big investment either way, but remember: if you want to install the program on more than one computer, you must buy a separate licensed copy for each computer. Otherwise, in most cases, you are breaking the law. And the homily "You get what you pay for" doesn't always apply here. We were unable to detect any clear relationship between price and quality.

Several publishers asked us not to include the prices of their software. At the same time, we realize that price is an important consideration for many readers. Therefore, we have designated the single-copy price as follows:

Low	Less than $100
Moderate	$100 to $400
High	$400 to $1000
Very High	Over $1000

ECSTATIC, VERSION 1.02

This program represents an interesting concept that we support wholeheartedly: it's cheap. We were unable to find any other general statistical program, except for public domain software, that sells for less. (STORM costs less, but it has a different range of features.)

ECSTATIC also is very easy to use. The menu options and prompts are self-explanatory and there is a convenient HELP file. The manual is well written, concise, and easy to read. The binding is simple, but attractive and durable.

The program was not designed specifically for forecasting, but it is readily adaptable for this purpose. It does single and multiple least squares regression, for example, and it prints some useful graphs such as histograms and scatter diagrams. There is a built-in variable called CASE# (case number) which you can use in trend line analysis, although the program doesn't do anything fancy like ARIMA modeling. ECSTATIC also displays the usual descriptive statistics, such as the mean and standard deviation, and it offers standard tests such as chi-square, Student's t, and analysis of variance.

If you want to use ECSTATIC for moving averages or exponential smoothing, then you have to get tricky. These procedures do not appear on the menu, but don't let fact stop you. There is a module called TR (for transformation) that enables you to write your own simple program. The syntax of the ECSTATIC language isn't too well documented, but it looks like a simplified version of BASIC or FORTRAN. The program can have up to 20 statements.

The intended purpose of the TR module is to create new variables or to modify existing ones, but you can do a lot in 20 statements. After experimenting with TR for a few minutes, we figured out a way to make the program calculate a three-month moving average and print the result. With a little more effort, it should be possible to write a file to do simple exponential smoothing the same way. (Hint: Use the LAG function.)

ECSTATIC might sound a little primitive by comparison with STAT-PAC GOLD and the other megapackages, but remember what we said earlier: studies have shown that the simplest forecasting methods often yield about the same level of accuracy as the more complex ones. The competence of the forecaster makes a much bigger difference than the price tag on the software. Also, future versions of ECSTATIC are expected to include more features, including an expanded programming language.

In summary, ECSTATIC is a good, inexpensive program with some limitations. It is available from:

SOMEWARE IN VERMONT, INC.
P.O. Box 215
Montpelier, VT 05602

Table 9-1. Key Features of Software Reviewed in Chapter Nine.

		Ecstatic	Forecast-pro	Lotus	Microstat	NCSS
I.	Options:					
	1. Judgmental/Scenarios[1]			X		
	2. Moving Averages				X	
	3. Exponential Smoothing		X		X	X
	4. Winters Method		X			
	5. Decomposition					
	6. Census X-11					
	7. Census Q-11					
	8. Adaptive Filtering					
	9. Kalman Filtering					
	10. ARIMA Modeling		X			
	11. Simple Regression	X	X	X	X	X
	12. Multiple Regression	X	X		X	X
	13. Box-Jenkins		X			
	14. ARARMA					
	15. MARMA		X			
	16. Spectral Analysis					
II.	Graphics Capability[2]		X	X		
III.	Flexibility[3]	X		X		
IV.	Cost (L, M, H, VH)[4]	L	H	M	H	M

Notes:

1. Actually you could use *any* program to test a scenario, just by entering data that is hypothetical rather than real. Lotus is just used more often for this purpose.

2. By "graphics capability" we mean significant high-resolution graphics. Most programs can print simple things like a histogram or scatter graph.

3. By "flexibility" we mean a built-in programming language that enables you to add procedures that aren't already included in the program.

4. Low = less than $100, Moderate = $100 to $400, High = $400 to $1000, Very High = Over $1000.

5. These programs are available in both scaled-down and standard versions, so the single-copy price varies.

Probe-PC	Shazam	Statgraphics	Statistix	Statpac-gold	Storm	Timestat	BMDP
		X		X			
X		X		X		X	
X		X		X	X	X	
X		X		X			
X				X			
				X			
							X
X	X	X	X	X		X	X
X	X	X	X	X		X	X
X	X	X	X	X	X	X	X
		X	X	X	X	X	X
		X		X			X
X	X	X		X			
X	X			X			X
VH	M	H	L	H	L/H[5]	L/H[5]	VH

FORECAST PRO

This is one of the few programs available that make the Box-Jenkins method really accessible to the nonmathematician. In addition, it is the only one we found that includes even a simple multivariate time series model (see chapter 7, MARMA).

The package runs in a fully automated mode, but it also enables you to override the resulting model if you think you can make better choices than the program does. In addition to Box-Jenkins and MAR (which they call "dynamic regression"), the package offers exponential smoothing, the Winters method, seasonal decomposition, and regression.

The FORECAST PRO manual comes in an attractive three-ring binder protected by a sturdy box. The content of the manual, however, is not the best we have seen. Each of the three sections has its own separate index, and two have their own glossaries. All of these are incomplete and ill-planned.

Some terms are defined in the text, others in the various glossaries, and still others in an appendix. Some terms are defined in several different places; others are not defined at all, and we could detect no pattern in these decisions. In addition, there are confusing footnotes that try to steer you to the right place, such as: "The autocorrelation function is defined in the appendix. The partial autocorrelation function is defined below."

The entire reference section glossary contains only nine entries, yet it has a technical error. It defines ARIMA as "Another word for Box-Jenkins." In reality, Box-Jenkins is only one way to develop an ARIMA model, and ARIMA is only one of the models used in Box-Jenkins. The indexes also are short, and are filled with typographic errors and surprising omissions of key terms.

Now that we are finished tearing apart the manual, we will readily concede that FORECAST PRO is a good program. The two disks contain most of the business forecasting techniques that you will ever need, together with an expert system that operates with little user intervention. There is an audit trail feature, which enables you to compare the results obtained with the various forecasting models. After you fit a model to your data, you can look at diagnostic tests that tell you how well the model is likely to work.

The program has full color graphics capability and can be used with a compatible printer or plotter. The installation procedure includes a number of convenient options; the program even asks whether you will tolerate screen flicker or not. (We could not get some of the installation options to work, however, even on a standard vanilla IBM PC. For example, we could not change the default data disk setting.)

The manual does have redeeming features. It contains a good tutorial section and a list of useful reference books and articles. The reference section contains fairly complete documentation of the statistical methods used.

One note about the expert system: this term generally means a program that mimics the decision-making processes of a human expert, in this case a forecaster. The accuracy of the result depends, therefore, on the skill with which the expert system has been developed and on the skill of the forecasters whose work is being emulated. We were not in a position to test the program at this level, but we have no reason to doubt its validity.

The price tag is in the high range, but FORECAST PRO might be well worth the investment if your company wants to use Box-Jenkins or multivariate time series analysis. As we explained earlier, very few businesses use these methods, despite their potential advantages, because they are extremely complicated. Unless you have a resident mathematician, and a highly competent one, your only real solution is an automated package like this. FORECAST PRO is published by:

BUSINESS FORECAST SYSTEMS INC.
68 Leonard St.
Belmont, MA 02178

LOTUS 1-2-3

Many business owners are already familiar with Lotus and similar spreadsheet programs. Spreadsheets are not designed just for forecasting, but they lend themselves to this purpose because they enable you to store and manipulate a lot of numeric data. They are particularly good for the "scenario" approach to judgmental forecasting, in which you compare the results of various assumptions regarding the next forecasting period.

Lotus is a mature and well-documented program with a versatile, ingenious design. Once the user has gotten well into the learning curve on the numerous facets of this program, it is easy to manipulate and format a variety of data sets. The package includes a complete built-in programming language. The graphics capability also is convenient and effectively augments the analysis of statistical data. Pie graphs, bar charts, line graphs, and other standard business graphics options are included.

The statistical functions available in Lotus allow handling of databases in a wide variety of combinations, limited only by the skill of the user and the available computer memory. Of particular interest in forecasting is the Data Table feature, which enables the user to create "what-if" scenario tables using one or two changing conditions. This feature allows rapid examination of the projected effects of various factors and makes clear the consequences of selecting a given path.

In addition to scenario analysis, Lotus is readily adaptable to standard quantitative forecasting methods. There are built-in functions which calculate the mean, standard deviation, and other standard descriptive statistics. The built-in Data Regression command makes regression analysis especially easy. With a sufficiently detailed macro (or program), Lotus can be be used to perform virtually any type of statistical or mathematical analysis.

The price of Lotus is in the moderate range, and it is published by:

LOTUS DEVELOPMENT CORPORATION
55 Cambridge Parkway
Cambridge, MA 02142

MICROSTAT-II, VERSION 1.02

MICROSTAT was introduced in the late 1970s and is said to be the most popular statistical package available for microcomputers. Longevity can be a good thing in itself, because it is a fairly good guarantee of continued product support. Also, by the time a program has been around for ten years, most of the major bugs have been eradicated and the manual has been tested in combat.

The version we reviewed (MICROSTAT-II, v. 1.02) runs like a well-oiled machine. Learning how to use it took us only a few seconds, as opposed to a few hours for some of the other programs reviewed here. The price is in the high range, however, and the program may do more than you need.

MICROSTAT-II, like STATGRAPHICS, includes most of the forecasting methods covered in our book: moving averages, exponential smoothing, and regression. The two packages are comparable in that both are fairly high-priced, general-purpose statistics programs. MICROSTAT-II runs faster than STATGRAPHICS and is far easier to learn, but it also offers somewhat less versatility. In the area of forecasting, for example, MICROSTAT-II doesn't include the Box-Jenkins procedure, the Winters method, or seasonal decomposition. A recent release (2.0) includes some new modules, but it still doesn't have these forecasting options.

MICROSTAT-II comes on three disks. You start the program by inserting Disk 1 and typing MSII at the operating system prompt. A horizontal menu line appears at the top of the screen, and from that point on it's all downhill. As you highlight each of the one-word options, the program displays a brief explanation. Function keys are defined on the screen when you need them. We were amazed at how easy it was to start using this program, even before we opened the manual. All the menu options and prompts are completely self-explanatory.

The MICROSTAT-II manual is readable and well indexed, and it comes in a sturdy three-ring binder. We did not find any major errors or problems in it, but then we didn't need to refer to it very often. Additions and changes to the manual are provided in the README file on Disk 1.

The program can be ordered from the following address:

ECOSOFT INC.
6413 N. College Ave.
Indianapolis, IN 46220

NCSS, VERSION 5.01

NCSS stands for Number Cruncher Statistical System. ("Number crunching" is a colloquial term that refers to processing large amounts of numeric data.) The program was first developed in 1982 and has an excellent reputation, although it appears to be aimed primarily at researchers, rather than business forecasters.

The NCSS base system comes on three diskettes labelled NCSS1, NCSS2, and NCSS3. To start the program, you insert the NCSS1 disk and type NCSS at the A> prompt. At that point you need to create a new database file or name an existing one, such as the SAMPLE file that comes with the program.

The first thing you get is a spreadsheet showing the contents of the database file. You can edit these values or leave them alone. When you are finished, you press the F10 key to display a menu of statistical options.

NCSS can do a great variety of statistics: mean and standard deviation (called descriptive statistics), contingency tables, ANOVA, single and multiple regression, discriminant analysis, and a lot of other things that we haven't talked about. The forecasting module, item H in the menu, is limited to time series analysis. If you want to develop a causal model you can select R from the menu, which covers regression and correlation.

The forecasting module enables you to do either simple least squares time series regression or exponential smoothing. In addition, the program has a special function that does moving averages. The ES options include the horizontal, seasonal, and both additive and multiplicative trend-seasonal models. NCSS makes you decide almost everything yourself, such as the values of the smoothing constants, so you really need to know what you are doing. The program displays an autocorrelation report, but it does not offer ARIMA models or the Box-Jenkins method. There is a convenient probability calculator, which displays various statistical tables.

In addition to the base system, NCSS has an optional graphics program, a student version, and two enhancement packages. We did not review any of these, but the advertisement for the graphics program states that it does *not* include standard business graphics such as pie charts and bar charts. This does not seem like a plus for a typical business user. On the other hand, the program does offer some unusual graphics that you might not find elsewhere (for example, you can amuse yourself for hours with Chernoff's Faces). One of the enhancement packages includes advanced multivariate techniques such as nonlinear regression and canonical correlation. The other package is for experimental design and quality control.

The NCSS manual is good except that it needs some proofreading. At one point, for example, the manual told us to insert the NCSS4 disk, and we were chagrined to find that there wasn't any. But most of the instructions are clear and concise, the print is easy to read, and the binding is attractive and durable. A disk file called README supplements the manual by describing any recent software changes. You need to know some statistics in order to understand the manual, but as we explained earlier, it's risky to use any forecasting program without some background knowledge.

The price of NCSS is quite modest. At the time this book was written, the price of the base system was in the low to moderate range, and the price of each of the other modules was in the low range. In addition, the publisher offers substantial quantity discounts. You can order the package from:

NCSS
865 East 400 North
Kaysville, UT 84037

PROBE-PC

This program, unlike many of those reviewed here, was designed specifically for time series analysis and forecasting. It includes not only a wide range of forecasting options but also a built-in report writer, graph writer, and programming language. The forecasting techniques available include moving averages, exponential smoothing, the Winters method, Census X-11 and Q-11, and several regression models. In addition, the program has color graphics capability. Surprisingly, however, PROBE-PC does not include Box-Jenkins analysis.

The PROBE-PC manual comes in a heavy-duty vinyl case that stands up well on a shelf and is impervious to spilled food and drink. It is profusely equipped with flip tabs, which are vital because the manual is fairly large. The Graph Writer chapter contains attractive full-color plates of sample output. The manual is very detailed and comprehensive, but it does not try to be a textbook. The explanations are quite technical and are aimed at experienced forecasters.

On the negative side, the version of the manual we received is a hybrid. The older sections are reminiscent of the standard IBM PC manuals, with glossy paper and crisp typeset lettering, but the updated sections are printed in small, indistinct type on a cheaper grade of paper. The manual also could benefit from the services of an editor. For example, the first sentence reads: "Here's introducing PROBE."

The regression package includes numerous options, such as Cochrane-Orcutt transformation, stepwise multiple regression, and curve fitting. It also includes two-stage and three-stage options for simultaneous equation models, which we did not discuss in this book.

In order to run the Census X-11 and Q-11 decomposition options of PROBE-PC, you need to have one additional piece of hardware in your computer called an 8087 math coprocessor. This is a chip that you can buy from a mail-order house and easily install yourself. As of this writing, the price of an 8087 is on the order of $100 to $300, depending on the type of system board in your computer. (Ask the dealer which type of 8087 you need.)

In summary, PROBE-PC is an excellent forecasting program designed for a user with a considerable background in mathematics and no specific need for the Box-Jenkins method. Its price is in the very high range, not including the added cost for the math coprocessor chip. The program is published by:

CONCURRENT TECHNOLOGIES
26 Broadway, Suite 1264
New York, NY 10004

SHAZAM, VERSION 6

We like the name of this program. The complete title is the SHAZAM Econometrics Computer Program. As this name suggests, the program was designed for causal modeling as well as the time series forecasting, and it seems to be aimed at professional economists and statisticians. It includes stepwise multiple regression, ARIMA modeling, high-resolution graphics, and a complete matrix capability. Despite this range of features, the price is in the moderate range.

We can't say much about the user manual, however, because we have not seen it. All we received was the abbreviated student version of SHAZAM, which is intended for use with a textbook, and a three-page description of the full program. Our review, therefore, is based mainly on the student version.

Unlike most of the programs we have reviewed, SHAZAM is command-driven, rather than menu-driven. That is, if you want the program to do something, you have to type out a specific command rather than select an option from a menu. This is hard to do without a manual that defines the commands, but we assume that a manual is available with the complete version of the program. You can also get a list of commands by using the HELP command.

The program comes with a demo, which consists of a series of paragraphs of text followed by simple exercises. These illustrate the use of a number of commands that enable you to read, display, and manipulate data.

The STAT command, followed by the appropriate variable names, a slash (/), and one or more modifiers, tells SHAZAM to execute a statistical procedure. Typing the command HELP STAT generates a list of these procedures, which include various descriptive statistics and tests such as ANOVA. There is also a command OLS which does ordinary least squares regression. Type HELP OLS for an explanation of this command.

In summary, SHAZAM appears to be a good program, but we are not in a position to say anything definitive about it. The user should be comfortable with basic statistical terms and with command-driven software. The program is published by a Canadian firm:

SHAZAM Econometrics Limited
12 Varsdale Place N.W.
Calgary, Alberta, Canada T2N 1N4

STATGRAPHICS*

STATGRAPHICS is a comprehensive statistical software package we have used for three years. The following review is based largely on STAT-GRAPHICS Version 1.1, but the publisher has kindly provided information regarding Version 3.0, released in December 1988.

The only major forecasting method that STATGRAPHICS does not include is adaptive filtering, and this might have been added by the time our book went to press. The program also generates an assortment of high-quality color graphics displays. Data can be typed at the keyboard or imported from an existing data file. The manual is large and well written, with generous flip tabs, and it stands up well on a shelf. User support is first-rate, and both the publisher and the software developer offer classes in the use of the program.

On the negative side, STATGRAPHICS is fairly expensive (in the high range), and it takes considerable effort to learn how to use it effectively. Version 1.1 runs very slowly on a standard PC, as compared with MICROSTAT and other programs. Version 3.0 is said to run faster, but the publisher still recommends that you use a PC/AT (which has a faster processor than a PC) for optimum performance. The main consideration, however, is that STATGRAPHICS may offer far more statistical power and versatility than your business will ever need.

The program comes on several disks (currently eleven). The old version required the user to answer a long list of questions about hardware; some of these questions made little apparent sense, but we

---

*STATGRAPHICS Statistical Graphics System is a registered trademark of Statistical Graphics Corporation, and is marketed exclusively by STSC, Inc.

learned to cope with them. The new version has an automated installation procedure with a separate Installation Guide to aid the user.

Before you start the program, we strongly suggest that you spend some time reading the documentation. The user manual is divided into chapters which correspond to the various program modules. All of these modules can be selected from the main menu by highlighting the appropriate title and pressing the Enter key. For the business forecaster, at least four different chapters are relevant (references are to Version 3.0):

Chapter 15, "Regression," covers the usual subject matter of least squares analysis. You access this module by highlighting "Regression" at the main menu. It can be used to develop single or multiple causal models. Stepwise and nonlinear options are included.

Chapter 16, "Forecasting," covers exponential smoothing, trend line analysis (simple regression), and seasonal decomposition. To execute these routines, highlight "Forecasting" at the main menu. The variations of ES include single, double (Brown's), and the Holt and Winters methods. In addition, this module enables you to fit product life cycle data to an exponential curve.

Chapter 18, "Smoothing," includes simple and weighted moving averages as well as some less common techniques that are not covered in our book (splines, polynomial smoothing, rate function estimates).

Chapter 19, "Time Series Analysis," includes the Box-Jenkins model fitting technique as well as several different methods of graphing and transforming data. The explanations are fairly detailed, and the manual walks you through a complete example involving sales data for champagne. The routine is not fully automated, however, and you need to understand how Box-Jenkins works in order to use it.

You can order STATGRAPHICS from the following address:

STSC, INC.
2115 East Jefferson St.
Rockville, MD 20852
1-800-592-0050
1-301-984-5123 (Maryland and Canada)

STATISTIX, VERSION 2.0

STATISTIX is a statistical software package that is often used by academic researchers. As a result, it does not offer the simpler forecasting methods such as exponential smoothing, which are useful mainly to business forecasters. Its time series module uses the Box-Jenkins technique. Our discussion in chapter 6 explained most of the terms and concepts that you will need in order to run this module.

STATISTIX does, however, use two terms that we did not discuss earlier: the *Marquardt criterion* and the *Nelder-Mead criterion*. The program asks you to specify a value for each, but the manual doesn't give you a clue as to what they are or how to select reasonable values for them. Again, the program is aimed at professional statisticians and their students, who are assumed to know what these terms mean already.

The Marquardt method is widely used for estimation of parameters in nonlinear regression problems. If you have some background in mathematics, we invite you to read the original paper by Marquardt.[6] But we promised not to talk about things like this in our book. There is no nonmathematical way to explain what these terms mean without sacrificing accuracy.

We recommend that you use a standard value for the Marquardt parameter (such as 0.001 or 0.0001) and skip Nelder-Mead altogether by typing *N* at that prompt. Then judge for yourself whether the results are satisfactory, by monitoring the forecasts that result.

The price of STATISTIX is in the low to moderate range, and we found it quite easy to use. As with most statistics programs, data can be typed in at the keyboard or read from an outside file. The manual is thorough and well written, although the print is tiny and the explanations assume that the reader already knows a lot about statistics.

In summary, STATISTIX is a fine program and very reasonably priced. It may not, however, be the ideal choice for a business forecaster with a limited mathematical background. The program is published by:

NH ANALYTICAL SOFTWARE
1958 Eldridge Ave.
P.O. Box 13204
Roseville, MN 55113

STATPAC GOLD, VERSION 3.0*

According to advertisements, a 1987 poll of *PC WORLD* magazine readers identified STATPAC GOLD as the world's best statistical and

---

*Not to be confused with another program called NWA STATPAK (spelled with a *k*). This is also supposed to be a good program, but it was not available for review.

forecasting package. After a brief review, we are inclined to agree with this assessment, although we do not necessarily recommend that you rush right out and buy the program. First, as always, figure out what your business needs and how much money you want to spend.

On the plus side, STATPAC GOLD is one of the most complete statistics packages available. It comes with an optional forecasting and quality control module which we highly recommend. This is the only program we have reviewed that includes adaptive filtering as an option. In fact, it includes almost every major forecasting method discussed in our book. Some of these procedures are hidden away, however, because the manual is not well indexed. That is, the index is large, but it is not well structured. (A few years ago, another reviewer complained that the STATPAC manual had *no* index.[5] It's gratifying to know that somebody listens to reviewers, even up to a point.)

Adaptive filtering, Box-Jenkins, exponential smoothing, and all your favorites are there, but many of them are not included as primary entries in the index. They are always subheadings of something else that you would never think of looking up unless you were already familiar with the program. A manual this big demands an adequate index. Also, the manual was irksome when it advised us to drink coffee and listen to music while working. We don't like coffee and we find music distracting.

Aside from these minor details, STATPAC GOLD is exceptionally well documented. The manual is clearly written and includes some very useful guidelines. It is more like a textbook than most other software manuals. Each procedure is explained clearly, with technical accuracy but with a minimum of awkward jargon. The binding is sturdy (although it's hard to open flat), and the print is easy to read. The appendices contain a fairly extensive bibliography and some useful statistical tables.

The structure of the program tends to discourage the casual reviewer. You can't just insert the disk and start punching away. In order to run some sample data, first we had to install more than two hundred files on our hard disk. (In practice, you would probably want to dedicate one microcomputer exclusively to STATPAC GOLD, especially if you have a lot of data files.)

Then we had to create a codebook file, a data file, and a procedure file. The codebook file describes the format of the data, such as the names, types, and locations of the variables. The data file contains the actual data. It can be a Lotus or dBase III file that you already have, so long as the STATPAC codebook file describes it correctly; or you can make a new file. The procedure file is essentially a batch file that tells the program what statistical procedures you want done.

These preliminary steps are less cumbersome than they may sound. Once you have created the three files, you can use them every month to run your forecasts. Forecasting tends to be a repetitive operation anyway, so this saves you time in the long run. All you need to do is edit the data files each month to reflect the most recent figures, and then run the forecast procedures that you have defined.

STATPAC GOLD has other nice features. Once it is installed, you can run many of the program options directly from DOS just by typing a single letter at the C> prompt. Also, the package includes a fine set of utility programs. One of these, for example, can adjust a time series data file to allow for holidays and other nonbusiness days. But you don't get all this for free. The price tag is in the high range by our definition, although it is less expensive than some comparable programs.

The software version that we reviewed is copy protected. You can make backup copies, but they won't work unless you call the publisher and get a password. Technical support is available by telephone, but only you or your designated assistant may call. There is also a detailed installation and deinstallation procedure to discourage you or your employees from stealing the program.

We found all this security inconvenient and somewhat silly. It's a forecasting program, for heaven's sake, not the blueprints for the Space Shuttle. The publisher states, however, that you can obtain a nonprotected version just by signing a legal agreement. We strongly recommend this option, assuming that your intentions are good.

STATPAC GOLD is published by:

WALONICK ASSOCIATES
6500 Nicollet Ave. S.
Minneapolis, MN 55423

STORM, VERSION 2.0

The manual describes this program as "an integrated software package consisting of the most frequently used quantitative modeling techniques for business and engineering problems." In its range of capabilities, STORM rivals some of the manufacturing management programs that sell for a lot more. We used Version 1.0 in our office for nearly three years and found it very satisfactory. Version 2.0, released in 1989, is even better.

Two different STORM packages are available: PROFESSIONAL STORM, priced in the moderate to high range by our standards, and PERSONAL STORM, priced in the low range. PROFESSIONAL STORM can handle more data, but otherwise the two programs are similar, and PERSONAL STORM would be enough for many small businesses. It's the least expensive of all the programs we have reviewed.

For example, the scaled-down program can analyze up to five time series at once, with up to 60 data values in each series—in other words, five different products for five years, assuming monthly sales figures. (If you have more than five products, you can easily create more than one data file.) PERSONAL STORM also would be an excellent choice for in-house corporate training programs, or for classroom instruction in any of several business subjects. PROFESSIONAL STORM will analyze prodigious amounts of data—for example, monthly sales figures for 1,000 different products for five years (or ten products for 237 years).

The program currently occupies three disks. You start by inserting Disk 1 and typing STORM at the A> prompt. The main menu lists sixteen software modules, as follows:

1. Linear & Integer Programming
2. Assignment
3. Transportation
4. Distance Networks (Paths, Tours, Trees)
5. Flow Networks (Max Flow, Transshipment)
6. Project Management (PERT/CPM)
7. Queueing Analysis
8. Inventory Management
9. Facility Layout
10. Assembly Line Balancing
11. Investment Analysis
12. Forecasting
13. Production Scheduling
14. Material Requirements Planning
15. Statistical Process Control
16. Statistics

When you pick a module, the program asks you to insert one of the other program disks. It's easier, however, to copy all the files to a hard disk and run the program from there instead. The software is not copy protected.

Many of these topics, such as inventory management, material requirements planning, and production scheduling, are directly related to the concerns of the typical business forecaster. Queueing analysis is a form of simulation that was mentioned in chapter 5. The STORM project management module is excellent; it does everything but yell at your employees for you. But most of these subjects are beyond the scope of this book, so your review is limited to the forecasting and statistics modules.

Forecasting, option 12, enables you to enter data or to type the name of an existing data file. The prompts that follow are easy enough, but the module includes only a single method—exponential smoothing. STORM is a good choice if you are a fan of this particular method, or if the nature of your data doesn't justify a more complex model.

The prompts are self-explanatory, with one minor exception. If you indicate that you want to create a new data file, the program displays the data entry screen, which asks you for the maximal length of any time series in the file. Now suppose you have one data value per month for a year. You type 12, obviously. Then you get another series of prompts, one of which asks you for the number of periods in a seasonal cycle (SEASON LNG). Logically, this answer also has to be 12 because there are 12 months in a year—but if you answer 12 to both questions, STORM won't do the analysis. Instead, it will tell you that the initial conditions cannot be fitted.

The reason is that the program uses an algorithm that requires the time series to be at least five (not three as the manual states) periods longer than the designated seasonal cycle. True, it would make no sense to try to fit a seasonal model with only a year of data, so this is a reasonable precaution. But STORM insists on having this much data even if you tell it to use the level (horizontal) model.

There are at least two solutions. You can wait until you have enough data values to satisfy the algorithm, 17 in this case; or you can enter 7 (i.e., 12 minus 5) at the SEASON LNG prompt, even though this may appear silly. But remember to specify a model other than seasonal when you get to the MODEL prompt (and a later menu that asks the same thing), or it will obediently fit a seasonal model based on a 7-month year. If you want a seasonal model, wait until you have two or three years of data.

The menus that come next enable you to edit, save, or print the data file, to modify various parameters, or to execute the forecasting module. All of these options run smoothly and create an impressive series of graphs, tabular displays, descriptive statistics, and forecast values. You can return to any previous menu just by pressing Esc as many times as necessary. The program can automatically select the model (level, trend, seasonal, or trend-seasonal) that best fits the data, as well as the best values for the smoothing constants. Or if you prefer, you can override the program and make these decisions yourself.

If your data set shows a definite trend, or if you are interested in developing a causal model, then you may decide to use the STORM statistics module instead, which you select from the main menu by typing 16. This module includes three options: data transformation, descriptive statistics, and regression analysis.

The first option enables you to compute new variables based on various combinations of existing variables. For example, if you have a data file that contains variables called PRICE and COST, you can compute a new variable called GROSSMARG by taking the difference of the two. The descriptive statistics option displays graphs and also computes the mean, variance, correlation coefficient, and similar things.

The regression option is the one that the forecaster is most likely to find useful. It can be used to develop both single and multiple regression models. For simple trend analysis, you would use just one independent variable with the integer values 1, 2, 3, and so on. PERSONAL STORM will accept up to ten variables (i.e., nine independent and one dependent) for 60 periods of data. As always, however, once you have a causal model, you have to understand how to use it to project a future value. This means being able to project likely future values for the independent variables.

The new STORM manual is very well done, with a sturdy binding and enough white space on each page to make the result readable. (Note, however, that the summary of features for each chapter appears on the page preceding the chapter. We looked all over the place before we found this important information.) The technical sections of the manual are very good, although they assume prior knowledge of the subject matter.

The following company publishes STORM:

HOLDEN-DAY, INC.
4432 Telegraph Ave.
Oakland, CA 94609
1-800-827-2665

TIMESTAT, VERSION 1.0

This is a brand-new software package for time series analysis, scheduled for release sometime in 1990. The publisher, Holden-Day (the same folks who brought you STORM), kindly allowed us to review a preliminary or "beta" version of the program.

At the time this review was written, a TIMESTAT user manual was not yet available. According to a preliminary manual written by the programmer, however, the program will offer an excellent range of time series analysis methods at a competitive price. Like STORM, TIMESTAT will be available in both scaled-down and standard versions. The former will be priced in the low range, by our definition, and will be adequate for many users. The full version will be priced in the moderate to high range.

The main menu for the student version includes the following:

- Box-Jenkins identification routines
- Box-Jenkins estimation/diagnostics/forecasting
- Stepwise autoregression (Box-Jenkins AR model)
- Exponential smoothing by Holt-Winters
- Single and multiple linear regression
- Input routine
- Edit routine
- Plot of raw data (to 8 series)

For each of these options, a corresponding function key (F1 through F8) prints a help message on the screen. In addition, the F9 key displays a Box-Jenkins tutorial and also explains data-input procedures for the program. The regression module offers curvilinear (non-straight-line) regression as well as the usual options.

It is clear that the software developer has done his homework and expects the user to do the same. For example, he tends to refer the reader to the classic 1976 book by Box and Jenkins. In principle this is a good idea, but the book isn't light reading and most business users would have trouble with it. (We feel it is mere coincidence that the book was published by the same company that publishes TIMESTAT.)

Reviewing beta software is always tricky. At this stage, for example, the TIMESTAT screen prompts and help messages need a little work. You would have to be a statistician to make much sense of them. And the program is far from idiotproof. When asked for the number of MA terms, you can type a number as large as five billion and TIMESTAT swallows it whole. Then it displays some zeroes and crashes, without a word of farewell.

By the time the program is on the market, all this will change. We predict that TIMESTAT will emerge as an excellent tool for students of time series analysis, as well as for business users with an average amount of training in statistics. It is amazing how much forecasting power and help information has been placed on a single disk, at a price anyone can afford.

The only real drawback is that TIMESTAT, unlike FORECAST PRO, does not run Box-Jenkins in a fully automated mode. You need to understand how it works, alas. This is a plus for students—at least from the viewpoint of the instructor—and a minus for everybody else.

TIMESTAT may be ordered from the following address:

HOLDEN-DAY, INC.
4432 Telegraph Ave.
Oakland, CA 94609
1-800-827-2665

FREE SOFTWARE

Most of the programs we have just reviewed are not very expensive. It costs more to hire a good consultant for a day or two than to buy most of these programs. But you can do even better than this.

If your budget is tight—or if you have plenty of money but prefer to spend it on something else—you can get your forecasting software absolutely free, or for a few dollars. We aren't recommending software piracy, which is a federal crime. We are referring to what is called *public domain software*.

Few people, other than hard-core computer freaks, realize how easy it is to get good programs that are not protected by copyright. If you know where to shop, you can get them for the price of a disk plus postage and handling—usually between $1 and $5. Some of these programs can be downloaded from computer "bulletin boards" that you access by modem.

There are also some similar programs called *shareware*, which initially you get for about the same price as public domain software. The difference is that, if you decide that you like the shareware program, you are then honor bound to pay a license fee at some point (usually about $25 to $75).

We have seen some fairly good public domain and shareware statistical programs, but there are too many to review individually here. If you can't find them, write to us in care of the publisher.

FIXING A COMPUTER

Most of the things that go wrong with a PC are easy to fix, even if you know absolutely nothing about electronics.

If one of your diskette drives stops working, for example, usually the best thing to do is to get a new drive and install it yourself. This is cheaper than walking in the door of most repair shops, and anyway a head alignment or cleaning is only a short-term solution.

At the time our book was written, mail-order firms were selling brand-new diskette drives for about $60. When ordering, make sure the new drive is the same size and type as the old one (half height or full height, 360K or 1.2 MB, 5-1/4 inch or 3-1/2 inch). Unplug the cables from the wall current, take the top off the computer, and study the existing drive to see how it is held in place. Then get a screwdriver and have at it.

```
            **WARNING**
     UNPLUG EVERYTHING FIRST
```

If your keyboard does funny things, probably it's dirty. We have gotten good results by jiggling the keys around or putting the keyboard in a warmer place for a while. Also, peer between the keys. If you see dirt, get the vacuum cleaner and vacuum it out. If you find peanut butter or other foreign matter, remove it, but don't get a lot of soap and water in there.

Another common problem involves the system board, or motherboard (the big board on the floor of the system unit). If an error message tells you that your system board is bad, or if it says something like GENERAL MEMORY FAILURE, your first step might be to call a computer repair shop. But hang up if they tell you that the motherboard must be replaced at a cost of several hundred dollars.

- You can buy a new PC-compatible motherboard for about $75 (without RAM chips) if you know where to shop.
- You can install it yourself without difficulty. You will need a screwdriver, as explained below, but probably you already have one of those or you couldn't have gotten the top off the computer.

- The chances are excellent that the whole motherboard isn't bad. Probably one or more of the RAM chips on it have blown. It's even cheaper and easier to replace the chip than it is to replace the whole board.

Electronic dealers sell RAM (random access memory) chips for about $10 each, depending on the type of chip and the current market. You can easily pull them out and replace them yourself. Find a dealer, tell her what kind of computer you have, and bring one of the old chips with you.

There is one other thing that you need to know about memory chips. A standard PC has two types of RAM chips, 64K and 256K. The numbers refer to the amount of memory on the chip. If your computer has 640K, then you might guess that it has only two of each type of chip: $(256 \times 2) + (64 \times 2) = 640$. But this isn't quite how it works.

Instead, you need a set of *nine* 256K chips to get 256K of memory. This is because there are eight bits in a byte, plus a parity bit, and each chip has one of the bits on it. The same holds true for the 64K chips. So there are 18 of each kind of chip on a motherboard with 640K. (You only need to replace the single chip that is bad, not the whole set.)

If you aren't sure where the RAM chips are, look at the picture in the computer manual. Or if you bought a really economical computer that doesn't include such amenities as a manual, just look around on the motherboard until you find an array of similar-looking chips. If you have 640K of memory on your motherboard, for example, you will probably see four rows of nine chips each.

If you don't know which chip is bad, just try replacing all of them, one at a time. Do this carefully to avoid bending pins. After each attempt, plug the computer in and try it. Unplug it before you try again. Eventually this procedure will lead you to the faulty chip. (You will know you have the right one when the computer starts working again.)

You don't need an IC puller to get a chip out. Just pry it up gently with a screwdriver. When you push the new chip in, be sure it is facing the same way as the others, and try not to bend any of the pins. If you bend one anyway, pull the chip out again and straighten the pin gently with your fingers or with a small pliers. If the pin breaks off, throw the chip away and buy another one.

If you have an extra memory card in your computer, it has RAM chips on it too, so the problem could be there instead of on the motherboard. In that case, leave the motherboard alone for the moment and try just taking the memory card out. If the computer works without it, you have found your problem. (Remember to change the switch settings on the motherboard to reflect the new amount of memory. Almost any computer comes with a manual that explains this much.)

You can either buy a new memory card (again, go to one of the cheap mail-order houses) or replace one or more of the memory chips on the one you have. Sometimes just vacuuming a memory board, jiggling it around, or letting it sit for a while will repair it. Once we left a bad memory board in a box for a year and it worked fine when we took it out again.

If two or three different chips are bad, you might think that all is lost, because you can't try every possible permutation. Wrong! You can buy a PC technical manual and try to decipher the error code that appears on the screen. Or you can just buy a complete set of new RAM chips (256K and 64K) and replace them all. You will need them eventually anyway, if your office has several computers. Then try putting back the old chips, one by one, and throw out the bad ones. Now you have some nice extra chips for the next time it happens.

If you do need a new motherboard after all, there is no reason to pay someone else to replace it. If you do this, you pay an unnecessary premium for the board itself plus at least $50 for labor. Some small repair shops will fix the board for a fraction of the replacement cost. Find one that will give you a free written quotation.

If the board can't be fixed for less than about $75, consider buying a motherboard from a discount dealer. Check the mail-order ads in the back of a computer magazine. When the board arrives, install it yourself. Save the RAM chips from the old board, if they were okay, and use them again.

Replacing the motherboard is easier than putting together a kid's toy or jigsaw puzzle. You don't need any tools other than a screwdriver, and you won't get electrocuted as long as you unplug everything first. Don't lose the screws.

```
**WARNING**
UNPLUG EVERYTHING FIRST
```

The only other repair problem we have ever had with our microcomputers involved the hard disk drive. On two occasions, suddenly a hard disk was completely inaccessible and seemingly destroyed. It turned out that there was nothing physically wrong with it. An electrical brownout or some mysterious act of God had simply erased part of the disk. We had to reformat the disk and start over.

If this happens to you more than once, you might want to buy a line power conditioner or voltage regulator. These devices eliminate changes in voltage that can damage your system. They cost about $150 and up, depending on how many computers you want to plug into the same device. (The inexpensive surge protector bars sold in electronics shops don't work very well.)

We are always hearing about hard disk crashes, although we have never had one. If you have reason to believe that a hard disk is *physically* damaged, and the warranty has expired, just buy a new one from a discount mail-order house and replace it yourself. Again, all it takes is a screwdriver.

SUMMARY

Hundreds of statistical programs are commercially available for microcomputers. These programs range in price from a few dollars to a few thousand dollars. Even if you are using one of the simpler forecasting methods, such as exponential smoothing, a program can save you a lot of time and effort. Routine maintenance of microcomputers is fairly simple because of their modular design.

REVIEW QUESTIONS

1. Is a computer system used for forecasting in your organization? If so, find out if it provides the output that the users want, and discuss some ways in which it might be improved.

2. Discuss some possible reasons why a business might decide not to use a computer for forecasting.

3. Can an expert system make a mistake? Explain.

ENDNOTES

1. C. Beaumont, E. Mahmoud, and V. E. McGee, "Microcomputer Forecasting Software: A Survey," *Journal of Forecasting* 4(1985):305-311.

2. H. V. Roberts, "Selection of Statistical Software for Micros," *Computers and the Social Sciences* 2(1986):65-68.

3. E. Mahmoud, G. Rice, V. E. McGee, and C. Beaumont, "Mainframe Specific-Purpose Forecasting Software: A Survey," *Journal of Forecasting* 5(1986):75-83.

4. E. Mahmoud, G. Rice, V. E. McGee, C. Beaumont, "Mainframe Multipurpose Forecasting Software: A Survey," *Journal of Forecasting* 5(1986):127-137.

5. L. O'Keeffe and J. Klagge, *Statistical Packages for the IBM PC Family* (New York: McGraw-Hill, 1986).

6. D. W. Marquardt, "An algorithm for least squares estimation of nonlinear parameters," *Journal of the Society of Industrial and Applied Mathematics* 11(1963):431-441.

Glossary

—William Shakespeare, *Love's Labor's Lost*

The jargon of forecasting is immense. This glossary is limited to the most common terms you are likely to encounter as a working forecaster, and yet it contains over 400 entries.

In statistics, familiar words often take on unfamiliar meanings that might not appear in standard dictionaries. Terms such as *normal, significant, robust, model, noise,* and *error* look innocent enough, but taking them at face value can be misleading. Some less common words, such as *spline,* also have unusual meanings in statistics.

Some of the definitions in this glossary are highly simplified to avoid long mathematical explanations. If you need a more formal definition, read the section of our book where the term is explained, or consult a statistics reference book.

ABC analysis As a general rule, a few products account for most of a company's sales. Forecast monitoring is most important for those products. Therefore, it is often useful to divide products into three groups: A (high turnover), B (moderate turnover), and C (low turnover). Hence the name ABC analysis.

absolute value To find the absolute value of a negative number, remove the minus sign. To find the absolute value of a positive number, leave it alone. The absolute value of X is denoted $|X|$.

AC 1. AUTOCORRELATION. 2. ALTERNATING CURRENT.

accuracy   In forecasting, the degree to which the predicted values match the actual data. (The term has a more specific meaning in statistics, but for our purposes it is essentially the same.)

accuracy ratio   Symbolized as $\overline{Q}$, the average value of Q for a set of data, where Q is a ratio between the forecast and actual value for a given interval. The ratio is constructed with the larger value (forecast or actual) on top. In other words, each value of Q is larger than 1.

ACF   Abbreviation for AUTOCORRELATION FUNCTION.

AD   Abbreviation for AVERAGE SIGNED DEVIATION.

adaptive estimation procedure (AEP)   One of several adaptive filtering methods used in business forecasting.

adaptive filtering (AF)   Any of several time series forecasting models that update their parameters continuously in an attempt to follow changes in the data.

adaptive response rate   A variation of exponential smoothing in which the algorithm determines the value for the smoothing constant at any given time, based on the error.

additive seasonality   A trend-seasonal pattern in which the magnitude of the seasonal fluctuations remains constant regardless of the level of the data. For example, as demand increases over time, the relative height of the seasonal peaks remains the same if this type of pattern is present.

AEP   Abbreviation for ADAPTIVE ESTIMATION PROCEDURE.

AF   Abbreviation for 1. AUTOCORRELATION FUNCTION. 2. ADAPTIVE FILTERING. 3. Air Force.

A/F Ratio   The ratio of the actual value to the forecast value.

after-the-fact forecasting   A method of testing a forecasting model. Another name for backcasting.

algorithm   A sequence of steps used to solve a given problem; usually refers to steps performed by a computer program.

alpha (α)   Greek letters such as α are used in mathematics to represent constants. In forecasting, it represents one of the following: (1) A confidence level. For example, a statistician might refer to an *alpha level* of 0.05. (2) The smoothing constant used in exponential smoothing. (3) The Y intercept, in the equation of a straight line. (Often this is represented instead by the English letter a.)

alternating current (AC)   A current that periodically alternates its direction of flow.

amplitude   In a cyclic time series, the distance between the peak and trough (high and low point) of the cycle.

analogous data   Sales data for a comparable product. Such figures often are used to generate forecasts on a new product that has no sales history.

analysis of variance (ANOVA)   A statistical procedure to test the significance of the results of other procedures, such as least squares regression. ANOVA tells you whether a significant amount of the variation in your data is explained by the model that you are using. (The goal of the model is to explain as much of the variation as possible.)

ANOVA   Abbreviation for ANALYSIS OF VARIANCE.

APE   Abbreviation for AVERAGE PERCENTAGE REGRESSION ERROR.

AR   Abbreviation for AUTOREGRESSIVE.

ARARMA   Abbreviation for AUTOREGRESSIVE AUTOREGRESSIVE MOVING AVER-
AGE.

ARI   Abbreviation for AUTOREGRESSIVE INTEGRATED.

ARIMA   Abbreviation for AUTOREGRESSIVE INTEGRATED MOVING AVERAGE.

ARMA   Abbreviation for AUTOREGRESSIVE MOVING AVERAGE.

arithmetic average   *See* AVERAGE.

association   *See* CORRELATION.

attribute data   Data that indicate the presence or absence of some attribute.
For example, the melting point of a screwdriver handle would be expressed as
a continuous variable, because it can take on any value in a continuous range of
numbers. The presence or absence of a hole for a key chain would be attribute
data. Either the hole is there or it isn't there.

autocorrelation (AC)   In time series data, the correlation between successive
data values. If autocorrelation is present, the data must be described by an
autoregressive (AR) model.

autocorrelation coefficient   Represents the strength of association between
successive values of the *same* variable.

autocorrelation function (AF)   A CORRELOGRAM: in time series analysis, a
plot of autocorrelations.

autoregressive (AR) model   A time series regression model that describes
the relationship between a dependent variable Y and several of its past values,
each of which is assigned a weight. Used when significant autocorrelation is
present.

autoregressive autoregressive moving average (ARARMA) technique
A method for selecting the time series regression model that best fits a given
set of data. Similar in concept to the Box-Jenkins approach but potentially easier to use.

autoregressive integrated (ARI) model   The model used for a nonstationary, nonseasonal time series that contains only AR parameters. Before the
ARI model can be used, the data must be differenced to achieve stationarity.

autoregressive integrated moving average model (ARIMA)   The model
used for a nonstationary, nonseasonal time series that contains both AR and
MA parameters. Before the ARIMA model can be used, the data must be differenced to achieve stationarity.

autoregressive moving average (ARMA) model   A time series regression
model used for a stationary, nonseasonal times series. It incorporates both the
autoregression (AR) and moving average (MA) elements. ARMA models frequently are used in time series regression analysis, especially in the Box-
Jenkins method. *See also* ARIMA.

average   (1) The arithmetic average, also called the simple average or
arithmetic mean. (2) Other measures of central tendency, such as the median
or mode. (3) A synonym for *typical*, as in the following sentence: "The
demand for widgets in an average month is 2,400."

average absolute percentage error   *See* MEAN ABSOLUTE PERCENTAGE
ERROR.

average error   *See* MEAN ERROR.

average percentage regression error (APE)   In a regression model, the standard error of the estimate (the actual outcome minus the forecast) divided by the actual outcome.

average signed deviation (AD)   The average (mean) of forecast errors, including both positive and negative values—which tend to cancel each other. Same as MEAN ERROR.

axis   One of the two perpendicular lines on a standard graph, called coordinates. The horizontal line is the X axis, and the vertical line is the Y axis. If three variables are being represented, there may be a third axis which looks as if it were sticking out of the page. This is called the Z axis.

backcasting or backforecasting   A method of testing a forecasting model before using it. First you develop the model based on past data, but you omit the data for a few past time periods. Then you see what the model would have predicted for those time periods.

backward stepwise elimination   The reverse of stepwise multiple selection. The procedure starts with all the variables in the model and eliminates them one at a time.

bar chart   A familiar type of graph, which represents the values of some variable on the X axis and the frequency (the number of data points with that value) on the Y axis. The frequency at each value is represented by the height of a rectangle or bar.

Bartlett's test   A test used in statistics to check for homoscedasticity, or the condition of having constant variance of the error terms in a model.

base index (BI)   With reference to seasonal data, the ratio between the mean value for a given season and the mean value for the year as a whole.

base series   A series of data values used in computing a base index.

batch processing   Submitting a list of instructions at one time, as in a disk file or stack of cards, and receiving the results at some later time. Compare INTER-ACTIVE PROCESSING.

best linear unbiased estimators (BLUE)   In regression analysis, coefficients derived by least squares.

beta (β)   A Greek letter used as a symbol in mathematics. In forecasting, it usually stands for one of the following: (1) The slope of a line; also represented by the English letter b. (2) A parameter used as an exponent to show how rapidly the standard deviation   (or the mean absolute deviation, in older programs) increases over time.

BFE   Abbreviation for BOLD FREEHAND EXTRAPOLATION.

BI   Abbreviation for BASE INDEX.

bias   In forecasting, some factor that causes estimates to be consistently higher or lower than they should be. For instance, if a polling organization wanted to determine the average income of Americans, but interviewed only homeowners in Orange County, California, the results would be biased.

binary notation   A way of representing numbers by using only two digits, 0 and 1.

binary variable   Another name for a DUMMY VARIABLE. It is called binary because it can have only two values, 0 or 1.

binomial distribution   A distribution that applies to data with the presence or absence of some attribute. A formal definition of the binomial distribution would require too much math for this book.

bivariate regression   A regression model with one dependent variable (Y) and one independent variable (X), or a multiple regression model with one dependent variable and *two* independent variables X_1 and X_2. In both cases, the model is *bivariate* because there are two variables, but in the first definition this refers to the total number of variables in the model, and in the second definition it refers to the number of X variables.

BLUE   Abbreviation for BEST LINEAR UNBIASED ESTIMATORS.

bold freehand extrapolation (BFE)   Forecasting by guesswork.

Box-Cox transformations   A set of transformations designed to make the relationship between two variables linear.

Box-Jenkins technique   A method for selecting the model that best fits a given set of time series data. The three basic types of models considered are the AR, MA, and ARMA models.

Box-Pierce Q statistic   A test used in the Box-Jenkins approach to time series analysis to test the autocorrelations of the residuals to determine whether the model fits the data; a variation of the standard chi-square test.

Brown's exponential smoothing   Another name for double exponential smoothing.

byte   A unit of measurement of the data storage capability of a computer.

calibration curve   A graph that shows the relationship between the actual value of something and the value as measured by an instrument that does not give completely accurate readouts (for example, an oven that is really hotter than the dial says).

Cartesian coordinates   The X and Y coordinates or axes on a standard two-dimensional graph.

categorical data   Data that fall into several categories, instead of following a continuous numeric scale. For example, a market survey might focus on individuals in several employment categories.

causal model   A mathematical model in which the X variables are causal factors rather than time. Sometimes, however, the same term refers to nonmathematical forecasting techniques that include considerations of cause and effect.

Census II, Census X-11, Census Q-11   Time series analysis methods developed by the Bureau of the Census, U.S. Department of Commerce, based on the decomposition technique. Census X-11 and Q-11 (the quarterly version) are the current versions as of this writing. *See* DECOMPOSITION.

central tendency   A way of expressing the typical or expected value of some variable with common measures such as the mean, the mode, and the median.

chi-square test   A statistical test to determine whether or not two or more groups of things differ significantly as to the frequency of some attribute.

Chow test   A statistical test to determine the structural stability of a regression model—that is, whether the relationships among the variables have remained fairly constant over time.

classical decomposition   *See* DECOMPOSITION.

cliometrics   The statistical analysis of historical data, as in econometric research.

Cochrane-Orcutt model   A type of moving average time series model.

Cochrane-Orcutt procedure   A statistical procedure used to transform data to eliminate autocorrelation.

coefficient   1. A number or symbol used as a multiplier of a variable. 2. A term more generally applied to various parameters such as the correlation coefficient or the coefficient of variation.

coefficient of determination   The formal name for R^2 (or r^2), the square of the correlation coefficient; used in causal forecasting models as a measure of the percentage of variation in the Y variable which is determined, or explained, by variation in the X variable.

coefficient of multiple determination R^2 for a multiple regression model.

coefficient of variation   A parameter calculated by taking the standard deviation of a data set and dividing it by the mean. The result is used as an index of the amount of variation in the data.

collinearity   A high level of correlation between two independent variables in a regression model.

combined forecast   A judgmental forecast obtained from a group of people rather than from a single individual.

confidence interval   A "plus or minus" factor used to bracket an estimate, often based on some multiple of the standard deviation.

confidence level   The level of confidence that you have in your interval forecast. Usually statisticians use the 95% confidence level, but sometimes the 90 or 99% level is used instead. (Note: If someone refers to the 5% confidence level, normally what he means is the 95% level. He is just looking at the problem from a different perspective.)

constant   In mathematics, a number that does not change (as opposed to a variable, which takes on many different values).

constant data   *See* HORIZONTAL DATA.

contingency table   A way of arranging certain kinds of data so that you can perform a chi-square test on them. A detailed example was presented in chapter 3.

continuous variable   *See* discussion under ATTRIBUTE DATA.

coordinate   *See* AXIS.

correlation   A statistically significant association between two variables. In other words, if two events or processes are correlated, then a change in one of them tends to be associated with a change in the other. The existence of a correlation does not imply that one event causes the other, nor does it explain the reason for the association. *See also* AUTOCORRELATION.

correlation coefficient (r or R)   A value that you calculate and then look up in a table in order to determine whether or not two variables are correlated. You may look up the formula in chapter 3 or leave it to your statistical program. The square of r is the coefficient of determination, q.v.

correlogram   A graph of a set of autocorrelations or partial autocorrelations, used to determine the time series regression model that fits a given set of data.

covariance   A parameter that reflects the degree to which two variables tend to vary together. (Computing this value is one step in computing the correlation coefficient.)

covariance structure model   A type of statistical model used to describe the relationships among a set of observed variables in terms of a smaller number of unobserved variables.

cross-impact analysis   A judgmental forecasting method that involves constructing a two-dimensional table of key factors that are relevant to the forecast. The forecasters then estimate the effect of each of these factors on every other factor.

cross-sectional regression   Another name for CAUSAL MODELING.

curve fitting   The process of determining the line that best describes or fits a given set of data, usually by means of least squares regression.

curvilinear regression   A regression model in which the line that best fits the data is curved rather than straight.

cusum chart   Stands for "cumulative sum" chart.

cusum signal   A forecast monitoring indicator which consists of the cumulative sum (cusum) of the forecast errors.

cycle stock   In inventory control, the average inventory level or the working stock.

cyclic data   A synonym for seasonal data, because seasons represent one type of cyclic pattern. Some books, however, draw a distinction between cyclic and seasonal components of time series data. By this definition, cyclic patterns are long-term fluctuations with a period of one to twelve years, whereas seasonal patterns occur within a year and are often equivalent to quarterly patterns.

data   The values of a variable; also called raw data. After data values have been rearranged or manipulated so that they tell you something that you want to know, they are called INFORMATION.

data transformation   Any process by which actual data values are converted to something else. For example, if you want to use the months of the year in a mathematical model, you must first convert them to numbers. Data values also can be converted to logarithms or transformed in various other ways.

decomposition   A forecasting technique to break down a time series into the following components: trend, seasonal, cyclical, and irregular.

DED   Abbreviation for deseasonalized demand. *See* DEMAND. *See also* DESEA-SONALIZED.

degrees of freedom   A number that is needed to determine the results of certain statistical tests. Chapter 3 explains the concept. Any computer program that does statistical tests can also find the degrees of freedom of the data.

Delphi method   A judgmental forecasting technique in which participants respond anonymously to a written questionnaire.

demand   The number of units of the product sold during a forecast interval, plus the number back-ordered. Sometimes a third factor, lost sales, also is added into the definition.

demand filter   A test that compares the actual current demand for a given item with the current forecast value. If the difference between the two (with any minus sign removed) is equal to a specified number of standard deviations, such as 4, a demand filter trip results. The new upper limit for the demand filter becomes the original forecast value plus the specified number of standard deviations.

dependent variable   The Y variable in a regression model. The name results from the fact that, in a causal model, the value of the Y variable is considered to *depend* on the value of the X variable(s).

DES   Abbreviation for deseasonalized sales. *See* DESEASONALIZED.

deseasonalized   Refers to a time series that has been smoothed to remove seasonal fluctuations.

deterministic model   A mathematical model that does not include an error term. Some authors, however, use the term to mean a causal regression model.

detrended   A time series that has been made stationary (the trend component is removed).

differencing   In the Box-Jenkins technique, the name of the process that makes the data horizontal (stationary).

discriminant analysis   A statistical method similar to multiple regression, except that the Y variable stands for an attribute rather than a measurement.

dispersion   In statistics, the amount of variation in a set of data. Some common measures of dispersion are the variance, the standard deviation, and the mean absolute deviation.

distribution free statistics   *See* NONPARAMETRIC STATISTICS.

disturbance   In forecasting, an unexplained factor that influences the data. The error term in a regression model is sometimes called the disturbance term.

double exponential smoothing   In exponential smoothing, if the data show a trend, it is necessary to apply the exponential smoothing operation twice.

double moving average   A moving average of values which are themselves moving averages.

double smoothed value (DSV)   The results of double exponential smoothing are called double smoothed values.

DSV   Abbreviation for DOUBLE SMOOTHED VALUE.

dummy variable   A variable that takes on one of two values, zero or one, depending upon whether a given condition is true or false. Such variables often are used in multiple regression or discriminant models.

Durbin-Watson test   A statistical test to detect serial correlation or autocorrelation.

econometrics   *See* MACRO FORECASTING.

econometric model   Any type of model used for macro forecasting. Sometimes, a system of linear multiple regression equations used for macro forecasting.

economic indicator   A variable that is a fairly reliable predictor of trends in the economy.

economic order quantity (EOQ)   In inventory control, the quantity of an item that must be ordered at one time to realize the lowest total cost. Often, EOQ is defined as the square root of the quantity *2dk/iv*, where *d* is the demand rate, *k* is the cost to place an order, *i* is the inventory carrying charge rate, and *v* is the unit value of the item.

efficiency   The efficiency of an estimator, such as the mean absolute deviation or standard deviation, is a measure of how good it is, relative to another estimator.

eighty-twenty (80-20) principle   The same concept as ABC analysis or the Pareto principle (q.v.), as applied to market forecasting.

elasticity coefficient   In a multiple regression model, to the percentage change in one variable divided by the percentage change in another variable. It is measured at the mean of each of the independent variables.

empirical   Based on observation rather than theory.

endogenous variable   In a forecasting model, a variable that depends at least partly on other variables that are included in the model.

EOQ   Abbreviation for ECONOMIC ORDER QUANTITY.

error term   In a regression model, the variation in the data not explained by the model. This error arises from two sources: unknown causal factors not included in the model; and random unpredictable disturbances.

estimation   The process of determining the approximate value of some parameter of interest by looking at a representative sample of the population. (A population, in this sense, is the entire group of things that you are interested in.)

EWMA   Abbreviation for EXPONENTIALLY WEIGHTED MOVING AVERAGE. Pronounced "YOO-ma."

ex ante   Before the fact; describes a procedure for testing the predictive value of a forecasting model.

exogenous variable   In a forecasting model, a variable that depends only on variables that are external to the system that the model represents.

expected value   In statistics, the average value to be obtained by infinitely repeated sampling. In general usage, the arithmetic mean or sometimes the mode.

expert system   A computer program that tries to emulate the decision making steps followed by a human expert in some field—a forecaster, for instance.

explanatory model   Another name for a causal model.

explanatory variable   Another name for an independent variable.

exponent   The power to which a number or variable is raised. In the expression X^2 or X squared, for example, the exponent is 2.

exponential growth   A pattern of increase that fits the model $Y = 2^X$. The graph curves sharply upward.

exponential smoothing   A time series technique in which the forecast for the next interval is based on a weighted average of the data for the previous *n* intervals. The weight is highest for the most recent interval, whereas those for earlier intervals decrease exponentially.

exponentially weighted moving average (EWMA) chart   A graph of values obtained through exponential smoothing. Pronounced "YOO-ma."

ex post   After the fact; describes a procedure for testing a forecasting model with past data.

extrapolation   Any method used to project a future value in a series of numbers, assuming that the series of values will continue to follow the same pattern that they have shown in the past. Essentially the same thing as time
series forecasting.

extrinsic forecasting   Another term for macro forecasting.

factor analysis   A type of statistical model which assumes that observed variables are generated by a smaller number of unobserved variables (called factors).

final forecast   By this method, a mathematical forecast is always combined
with the judgment of a manager or other decision maker. In practice, if the two
are at odds, this can be a difficult proposition.

FORAN   Abbreviation for FORECAST ANALYSIS.

forecast   As used in this book, any attempt to predict future events.

forecast analysis (FORAN)   A flexible sales forecasting method developed in
the 1960s by Robert L. McLaughlin. It is related to seasonal decomposition
but can be used for both causal and time series models.

forecast error   The difference between the forecast value and the actual value.
Same thing as residuals.

forecasting system (FORSYS)   A forecasting method used extensively in
Europe. It is said to be similar to the Winters method of exponential smoothing, except that the three parameters used in the model are derived differently.

forecast interval   The period of time for which a forecast is made. If you are
trying to predict monthly demand for a product, for example, the forecast
interval is one month.

FORSYS   Abbreviation for FORECASTING SYSTEM.

forward stepwise selection   Another name for stepwise multiple regression.

frequency   In a cyclic time series, the length of time between one cycle and the
next.

F test   A test used to compare two variances, to see whether there is a statistically significant difference between them.

fudge factor   A correction factor of any kind, but often one that is applied sur-
reptitiously. For example, if you know that your forecasting program tends to
underestimate the actual demand for a product by about 10%, but you don't
know how to fix it properly by changing the settings, you might take the program output and manually add a fudge factor of 10%.

function   A relationship between two or more variables. As one variable
changes, the function dictates that the other also must change in accordance
with a given pattern. The statement $Y = f(X)$ reads "Y is a function of X."
This means the value of the dependent variable Y changes in response to
changes in the value of the independent variable X.

futuribles or futuristics   *See* LA PROSPECTIVE.

GAF   Abbreviation for GENERALIZED ADAPTIVE FILTERING.

gamma (γ)   A Greek letter that, in forecasting, usually stands for a smoothing
constant used in certain variations of exponential smoothing.

generalized adaptive filtering (GAF)   A version of adaptive filtering that
incorporates the concept of autocorrelation.

generalized exponential smoothing (GES)   An extension of the exponential smoothing method.

generalized least squares (GLS)   The process of transforming data and then applying ordinary least squares analysis to the transformed data.

general-purpose simulation system (GPSS)   A widely used high-level computer simulation language suitable for many business applications, including the development of queueing models.

geometric average (geometric mean)   To find the geometric average of a series of numbers, either (1) find their logarithms, calculate the mean of these values, and then transform the result back to an ordinary number by finding its antilogarithm; or (2) multiply together all n values in the series and then find the nth root of the product.

geometric growth   A pattern of increase that fits the general model $Y = X^2$. Instead of *being* an exponent, as in exponential growth, X *has* an exponent. Again, the graph curves sharply upward but the shape is different.

GES   Abbreviation for GENERALIZED EXPONENTIAL SMOOTHING.

gigabyte   One thousand megabytes, or 1 billion bytes. A measure of the amount of data that a computer can accommodate.

GLM   Abbreviation for GENERAL LINEAR MODEL.

GLS   Abbreviation for GENERALIZED LEAST SQUARES.

GNP   Abbreviation for GROSS NATIONAL PRODUCT.

Goldfeld-Quandt test   A statistical test used to check for the presence of homoscedasticity, or the condition of having constant variance of the error terms in a model.

goodness of fit   In statistics, the degree to which a proposed model or probability density function fits some data. There are various tests for measuring goodness of fit. Some of them are described elsewhere in this Glossary.

GPSS   Abbreviation for GENERAL-PURPOSE SIMULATION SYSTEM.

graph   Data represented in pictorial form; also called a plot or chart. Chapter 3 describes various types of graphs.

gross national product (GNP)   A measure of the national income which includes all goods and services produced.

harmonic series   A time series that involves two trigonometric functions called the sine and cosine.

harmonic smoothing   A method of time series analysis that is used with harmonic series.

heteroscedastic   Describes a variable for which the variance is not the same across the range of observed values.

heuristic   Involving a trial-and-error approach to problem solving.

histogram   A graph similar to a bar chart, except that the bars usually are drawn as thin lines, and they often run horizontally on the page, rather than vertically as in a bar chart.

Holt's exponential smoothing   A double smoothing technique.

homoscedastic   Describes a variable for which the variance is the same across the range of observed values.

horizontal demand   A pattern of product demand that is more or less constant from one forecast interval to the next. The pattern does not show evidence of a trend (increase or decrease) or seasonal fluctuations. It is called horizontal because, if you graph the data, the resulting line runs more or less horizontally across the page. This pattern is also called stationary, level, or constant.

horizontal-seasonal demand   A pattern of demand that includes both horizontal and seasonal components. That is, demand varies in a predictable manner from one season to another, but the overall demand from one year to the next is about the same.

IMA   Abbreviation for INTEGRATED MOVING AVERAGE.

immediate-term forecast   Forecasts of events less than one month in the future. Other authors prefer to combine this category with short-term forecasts.

independent variable   In a regression model, the X variable (or one of several X variables in a multiple regression model). Also called a predictor variable or explanatory variable.

industry forecasting   Another name for technological forecasting.

information   Raw data that has been processed in some way that makes it meaningful to the user.

initialize   To assign initial values to some parameters that a forecasting system will use. For example, if your system will use the moving average technique, you need to tell it how many intervals of data to use in computing the forecast.

input-output analysis   A forecasting technique used in generating macro forecasts and econometric models. It views the economy as an interrelated system in which the sales (output) of one industry are the purchases (input) of another industry. Thus it seeks to determine the amount of goods and services that must be input to this system in order to meet consumer demand.

integer   A number without a decimal part. For example, 2, 37, and 1,400 are integers; whereas, 2.0, 37.3, and 1,400.25 are not integers. In computer terminology, this term also refers to the way the computer represents numbers internally.

integrated moving average (IMA) model   The model used in time series analysis for a nonstationary, nonseasonal series that contains only MA parameters. Before the IMA model can be used, the data must be differenced to achieve stationarity.

interactive   Describes a computer program that enables the user to interact with the analysis process by typing an instruction at the keyboard and obtaining a response shortly thereafter.

intercept   The point at which a regression line crosses the Y axis of a graph. In the equation of a line, the intercept (also called the Y intercept) often is represented as a.

intermediate forecast   Forecasting for a period of three months to two years in the future. Also called medium-range forecasting. The definitions vary considerably, however, from one book to another.

interpolation   The process of computing a missing value within a series (as opposed to extrapolation, in which you find the next value after the end of a series).

interval forecast   A forecast that includes a confidence interval, as in the following statement: "The expected demand for widgets in April is 5,200 plus or minus 730."

intervention model   A type of transfer function model that contains a dummy variable as one of the independent variables.

intrinsic forecasting   Another name for micro forecasting.

inventory management   The process of determining optimum order quantities and order times in relation to the costs associated with ordering and maintaining inventory.

inverse correlation   A relationship in which the value of one variable decreases as the value of another variable increases. The result is that the trend line slopes downhill.

irregular factors   The random component in a decomposition model.

irregular fluctuation   *See* LUMPY DEMAND; NOISE.

JEO   Abbreviation for JURY OF EXECUTIVE OPINION.

judgmental correction   Another name for a fudge factor. A correction applied to a forecast, based on human judgment.

judgmental forecasting   Forecasting based on human judgment rather than on a mathematical technique.

jury of executive opinion (JEO)   A judgmental forecasting method in which a group of managers hold a meeting to arrive at a consensus forecast.

K   In forecasting, the learning constant used in adaptive filtering. It can also stand for a constant in an exponential growth equation. With reference to computers, it means the number 1024.

Kalman filtering   An adaptive forecasting technique used for estimating parameters in time series analysis.

kilobyte   One thousand bytes; actually 1024 bytes.

kludge   1. An affectionate term for a computer. 2. A pasted-together but working system of any sort. Pronounced "klooj."

Kolmogorov-Smirnov statistic   A test to determine whether a set of data has a normal distribution or not.

ladder chart   A type of chart used in forecast monitoring. It includes graphs of monthly forecasts, actual values, and the five-year average, minimum, and maximum value.

lag   In a time series, the length between time periods. For example, an autocorrelation of two lag periods means the relationship between periods 1 and 3, periods 2 and 4, and so forth.

la prospective   A long-term forecasting method developed in France. This school of thought, to quote Wheelwright, "advocates active participation in the creation of the future." This is too weird for us.

last period forecasting   Another name for the naive model or random walk model.

lead time   The length of time expected to elapse between a decision and its result (for example, between ordering an item and receiving it).

learning constant   A parameter K used in adaptive filtering.

least squares regression   *See* REGRESSION.

level time series   Another name for a horizontal time series.

linear dependency   An exact linear relationship between two variables.

linear exponential smoothing   Another name for double exponential smoothing, used when there is a trend in the data.

linear moving average   Another name for the double moving average method.

linear regression   A straight-line regression model. Also called a line model.

LISREL   The name of a computer program used in estimation of the covariance structure model—a topic not covered in this book. The name is also applied to the technique which the program uses.

logarithm   An exponent indicating the power to which a number must be raised in order to produce a given number.

logistic regression   Another name for probit regression, except that it uses a different distribution (the cumulative logistic distribution). It is a variant of discriminant analysis in which the outcome variable takes on only two values, 0 or 1.

long-term forecast   A forecast of events more than two or three years in the future, depending on the author's definition.

lumpy demand   A pattern of product demand that fluctuates over a wide range from one forecast interval to another, but which shows no evidence of a predictable seasonal pattern.

MA   Abbreviation for MOVING AVERAGE.

macro forecast   A forecast that pertains to national or world economic conditions; sometimes called an economic forecast or extrinsic forecast. Compare micro forecast.

MAD   Abbreviation for MEAN ABSOLUTE DEVIATION. (Some books define this as MEAN AVERAGE DEVIATION instead, but it amounts to the same thing.)

MAPE   Abbreviation for MEAN ABSOLUTE PRECENTAGE ERROR.

market share   The proportion of the total market that is claimed by a certain company or product line.

Markov chain   A model in which the probabilities for a set of events create a new set of probabilities for later events. *See* chapter 5.

MARMA   Abbreviation for MULTIVARIATE AUTOREGRESSIVE-MOVING AVERAGE MODEL.

mathematical model   *See* MODEL.

mathematics   The branch of science which deals with quantities, forms, and similar concepts by means of numbers and symbols. (Statistics is one area of applied mathematics, whereas quantitative forecasting is one area of statistics.)

matrix   In mathematics, a two-dimensional table of numbers that can be manipulated according to certain rules.

maximax   An expression which simply means selection of a strategy that is likely to maximize profit, without consideration of risks involved. *See* MINIMAX.

maximin   A statistical method used for assigning numeric scores to data classifications. Oddly enough, this has nothing to do with either Maximax or Minimax.

MCD   Abbreviation for MONTH FOR CYCLIC DOMINANCE.

ME   Abbreviation for MEAN ERROR.

mean   The arithmetic average of a set of data.

mean absolute deviation (MAD)   Like the standard deviation, an estimator of the square root of the variance. (More precisely, it is an estimator of about 0.8 times the square root of the variance. In other words, 1.25 times the mean absolute deviation is about equal to the standard deviation.)

mean absolute percentage error (MAPE)   A method, like standard deviation and mean absolute deviation, for estimating variation. You take the absolute value of all the percentage errors for a set of data and then find the mean of these values.

mean error (ME)   The mean forecast error, including both positive and negative error values, which tend to cancel each other. Same as average error, average signed deviation, et alia.

mean percentage error (MPE)   The mean of all the percentage errors for a set of data.

mean squared deviation error (MSD)   Another name for the variance.

mean squared error (MSE)   Another name for the variance.

medial average   Term used in connection with the development of seasonal index factors in forecasting. It is determined by dropping the highest and lowest ratios from each of the four quarters, and then finding the average of the remaining ratios. The purpose of this step is to eliminate extreme values.

median   The midpoint of a set of data. In other words, the number of data points smaller than the median will be equal to the number of data points larger than the median.

medium-range forecast   Another term for an intermediate forecast.

megabyte   One million bytes.

micro forecast   A micro forecast, also called an intrinsic forecast, is related to a company's own unique requirements. A macro forecast, by contrast, pertains to national or world economic conditions.

minimax   Mickey's girl friend or a sales strategy in which management tries to commit as few major blunders as possible.

missing values   Literally, data values that are missing from a set of data. Most major statistical programs include procedures for dealing with missing values.

mixed model   A time series model that combines AR with MA. An ARMA or ARIMA model, depending on stationarity.

mode   In a collection of data values, the value that occurs most often. *Compare* MEAN and MEDIAN.

model   By the definition used in this book, a model is a mathematical representation of the relationship between two or more variables.

Monte Carlo method   A common method of simulation which involves the use of a random number table or a computer language with a built-in random number generator. This book does not deal extensively with simulation, so we will not discuss this method in detail. Most comprehensive textbooks on business mathematics explain how Monte Carlo simulation works.

month for cyclic dominance (MCD)   In the Census decomposition forecasting methods, the ratio between the mean percentage change in the random component and the mean percentage change in the trend/cycle component.

moving average (MA)   (1) A time series method in which the arithmetic mean of the data for the previous n forecast intervals is used as the forecast for the next interval. (2) A time series model in which there is autocorrelation between the error terms for successive forecast intervals.

MPE   Abbreviation for MEAN PERCENTAGE ERROR.

MSD   Abbreviation for MEAN SQUARED DEVIATION.

MSE   Abbreviation for MEAN SQUARED ERROR.

multicollinearity   In multiple regression, a high level of correlation among the independent variables. This situation causes problems with the model, so it is best to select X variables that are not highly correlated with one another.

multiple regression   Regression analysis in which there are two or more independent (X) variables. Also called multivariate regression.

multiplicative seasonality   A trend-seasonal pattern in which the magnitude of the seasonal fluctuations depends on the level of the data. For example, as demand increases over time, the relative height of the seasonal peaks also increases if this type of pattern is present. *See* ADDITIVE SEASONALITY.

multivariate analysis   Any method of statistical analysis which involves more than two variables. Multiple regression and discriminant analysis are examples.

multivariate autoregression-moving average (MARMA) model   A regression model that combines the features of time series and causal models.

multivariate regression   *See* MULTIPLE REGRESSION.

naive forecast 1 (NF1)   Another name for the naive or random walk model.

naive forecast 2 NF2   This is the same as NAIVE FORECAST 1 (NF1) except that the data values are first adjusted for seasonality.

naive model   A forecasting model that states changes will not occur from one forecast interval to the next. It is also called a random walk model, or the last period forecasting technique.

NF1   Abbreviation for NAIVE FORECAST 1.

NF2   Abbreviation for NAIVE FORECAST 2.

noise   In the statistical sense, random unexplained error or variation in the data. Sometimes it is called white noise.

nonparametric statistics   Statistical tests used when the distribution of the data is not known or does not meet the requirements of a more commonly used test.   Also called distribution-free methods.

nonstationarity   The condition when data are *not* stationary.

nonstochastic model   *See* STOCHASTIC MODEL.

normal distribution   A bell-shaped pattern that appears when you draw a frequency plot for many kinds of data.

null hypothesis   This concept is explained in more detail in chapter 3. Briefly, the null hypothesis is a way of setting up the question that a statistician wants to ask. Then a test is performed to find out whether the null hypothesis is likely to be true or false.

observation   A data point; an observed value of a variable.

ordinary least squares (OLS)   For our purposes, this is the same thing as simple linear least squares regression.

optimal weights   (1) The best values for weights used in any model. (2) The final weights used in adaptive filtering.

order (of a time series regression model)   The number of terms in the model, usually designated as p for AR models and q for MA models.

origin   On a graph with X and Y coordinates, the origin is the point $(0,0)$ at which the two coordinates cross each other.

outcome variable   Another term for the dependent (Y) variable in a regression model.

outlier   A data value that is far outside the expected range. Whether or not such values should be thrown out, however, depends upon how the "expected range" was determined.

PAC   Abbreviation for PARTIAL AUTOCORRELATION.

PACF   Abbreviation for PARTIAL AUTOCORRELATION FUNCTION.

panel forecasting   Forecasting done by a committee that includes panel members from several different industries, usually under the aegis of some outside organization.

parameter   Like many other terms borrowed from mathematics, such as model and simulation, this one has become a buzz word in business. Managers who wish to appear erudite will speak of the parameters of a situation. As used in statistics or computer programming, however, the term refers to a numeric value such as a constant or a coefficient.

Pareto principle   Same concept as ABC analysis, as applied to production data.

partial autocorrelations (PAC)   A set of statistical measurements that are similar to autocorrelations. They are used for determining the number of AR parameters in a Box-Jenkins model.

partial correlation   Suppose that you have a model with three X variables: X_1, X_2, and X_3. If your computer printout identifies a value as the partial correlation coefficient $r_{12.3}$, it means the correlation that exists between variables X_1 and X_2 when variable X_3 is held at a constant value.

partial regression coefficient   One of the regression coefficients (b_1, b_2, etc.) in a multiple regression model.

peak   A high point on a time series graph of cyclic or seasonal data.

Pearson's product-moment correlation coefficient   Another name for the correlation coefficient, r.

periodicity   The quality of having a regularly recurring cyclic pattern.

pie chart   A popular type of graph that is used to represent categorical data. A circle is divided into several wedge-shaped sections, each of which is proportional to the percentage of data points that fall into the category represented by that wedge.

plot   A graph that displays individual data values. Most other types of graphs are smoothed in some way.

point forecast   A forecast consisting of a single number, as opposed to an interval forecast, which is a range of values within which the true value is expected to fall.

Poisson distribution   A distribution used with attribute data, such as the number of defective items in a sample, and encountered in connection with queuing models. For a formal definition consult a math book.

polynomial   In mathematics, an expression that contains two or more terms, such as the equation of a line.

population   The entire group of things or events that the statistician is working with.

population variance   *See* VARIANCE.

POQ   Abbreviation for PRODUCTION ORDER QUANTITY.

prediction   In this book, any attempt to estimate future events.

prediction-realization diagram   A scatter diagram that shows the relationship between forecast values and actual values; used to determine how well a forecasting method is performing.

predictor variable   Another name for an independent (X) variable in a regression model.

primary data   Data collected specifically for the purpose at hand. Secondary data, by contrast, are data that were collected for some other purpose but later re-analyzed.

probability   The likelihood of occurrence of a given event, usually expressed as a fraction or percentage.

probability statement   Any statement of the mathematical probability of some event.

probit regression   Same thing as discriminant analysis, but with only two possible values for the outcome variable (0 or 1).

production order quantity (POQ)   In inventory control, the quantity of an item that you must manufacture per batch in order to realize the lowest total cost. It is similar to EOQ, except that EOQ assumes the items will be ordered rather than manufactured internally. Often, POQ is defined as the square root of the quantity $2dkp/iv(p-d)$, where d is the demand rate, k is the cost to place an order, p is the production rate, i is the inventory carrying charge rate, and v is the unit value of the item.

product life cycle   A model of product demand which can be graphed as an S-shaped curve. The model assumes that demand first grows slowly, then rapidly, then levels off.

projection   Another name for extrapolation.

prospective approach   *See* LA PROSPECTIVE.

proxy variable   In a causal model, a variable that you substitute for something else that is harder to measure.

Q-statistic   A statistical test used to detect autocorrelation.

quadratic model   A model with a second-degree term in it (a squared term). The trend line for such a model curves upward. *See*, for example, GEOMETRIC GROWTH.

qualitative   Subjective; judgmental. A general approach to the interpretation of data that says nothing about the validity of the results.

qualitative forecasting   Another name for judgmental forecasting.

quantitative Objective; mathematical. A general approach to the interpretation of data with no implications regarding the validity of the results.

quantitative forecasting Forecasting that makes use of mathematical models.

queuing model Also called a waiting line model, this is a type of mathematical model often used in business applications. The name may derive from the fact that businesses often use it to predict how many people are likely to be standing in line at any given time, given a specified set of conditions. A computer program called GPSS is often used for developing this type of model.

R or r: *See* CORRELATION COEFFICIENT. Sometimes, *R* is used for the multiple correlation coefficient and *r* for the single correlation coefficient.

R² or R squared *See* COEFFICIENT OF DETERMINATION.

ramp model A model that shows an upward trend, or specifically a steady upward trend.

random Unpredictable. When applied to a series of numbers, this term means that any number within a specified range has an equal probability of being the next one to occur in the series. When applied to error in a regression model, it means error that could not be predicted by the model.

random sampling A sampling method designed in such a way that every item has an equal chance of being selected.

random walk model Another name for the naive model.

randomless A strange way of saying "nonrandom," which, of course, means not random.

RD Regular differencing. *See* DIFFERENCING.

reciprocal One divided by a certain number. When you multiply a number times its reciprocal, you get 1. For example, the reciprocal of 5 is $1/5$ or 0.20.

recursive model A mathematical model that involves a series of repetitive calculations, each of which depends upon the result of the previous repetition. For example, exponential smoothing is called a recursive model because it builds on the results of previous calculations.

regression Any of several methods for drawing or calculating the line which best describes a given set of data. Usually it means least squares regression, which seeks to minimize the sum of squared forecast errors.

regression coefficient In a regression model, the beta or *b* value which represents the slope of the line.

regular AR model *See* AUTOREGRESSION.

regular MA model *See* MOVING AVERAGE.

residuals In regression, the distances between the regression line and the actual data values. In other words, the residuals are the differences between the forecast values and the actual values, so they tell you how much of the variation in the data is not explained by the regression model.

response variable Another name for the dependent or outcome (*Y*) variable in a regression model.

rho (ϱ) A Greek letter that is often used as a symbol for the autocorrelation parameter.

robust   Reliable, regardless of the distribution of data values. The Student's t test, for example, is said to be robust because it works even if the data depart from the normal distribution.

root mean square error   *See* STANDARD DEVIATION.

rounding   Simplifying a number with a long or repeating decimal, or a number that simply has a higher degree of precision than you want. For example, 3.141592 could be rounded to 3.1416 or to 3.14, depending upon the precision needed. 100,000,037 might sound better as 100 million in certain contexts.

SABL   Abbreviation for SEASONAL ADJUSTMENT, BELL LABORATORIES.

safety stock   The extra amount of a product that you keep in stock in order to allow for unexpected events, such as delays in delivery schedules or customer demand that is higher than expected.

sales force forecasting   A judgmental forecasting method based on the estimates of a group of sales personnel.

sample   In statistics, a number of items selected at random from a population so as to be representative of that population.

sample variance, sample mean, etc.   Estimates of the true population variance, mean, and so on, based on observations of a representative sample.

sampling error   The random, unavoidable differences between a sample and the population it is supposed to represent.

SAR   Abbreviation for SEASONAL AUTOREGRESSIVE.

SARIMA   Abbreviation for SEASONAL AUTOREGRESSIVE INTEGRATED MOVING AVERAGE.

SARMA   Abbreviation for SEASONAL AUTOREGRESSIVE MOVING AVERAGE.

scatter diagram   A two-dimensional graph showing individual data points; also called a scatter graph, scatter plot, or scattergram. Drawing a scatter diagram is a useful first step in analyzing many kinds of data.

scenario   An imaginary future situation, as used in judgmental forecasting.

S-curve   A type of graph that describes certain phenomena, such as the product life cycle.

SD   Abbreviation for seasonal differencing. *See* DIFFERENCING.

seasonal adjustment, Bell Laboratories (SABL)   A seasonal decomposition procedure.

seasonal autoregressive integrated moving average model (SARIMA)   A time series model. *See* ARIMA.

seasonal autoregressive (SAR) model   A time series model.

seasonal autoregressive moving average (SARMA) model   A time series model. *See* ARMA.

seasonal data   A pattern of data values that vary significantly and consistently from one season to another. In the case of seasonal demand for a product, some forecasters also stipulate that there must be an identifiable *reason* for the pattern.

seasonal index   *See* BASE INDEX.

seasonal moving average (SMA) model   Used in time series analysis. *See* MOVING AVERAGE.

secondary data   Data that were collected for one purpose but later re-analyzed for another purpose. Primary data, by contrast, are data that were collected specifically for the application at hand.

SEE   Abbreviation for STANDARD ERROR OF THE ESTIMATE.

serial correlation   Another name for autocorrelation.

service level   The percentage of orders which a company is able to fill. If you receive 100 orders for an item but you are able to supply only 95 of them, the service level for that item is 95%. In the other five cases, you ran out. One of the main reasons for forecasting is to prevent those stockouts from happening.

short-term forecast   In this book, a forecast of events up to three months in the future. In some books that include immediate-term forecasting as a category, short-term forecasting refers to events one to three months in the future. In others, short-term forecasting covers intervals up to a year.

significance   In statistics, if a test result is said to be significant at (say) the 95% confidence level, this means that 95 times out of 100 a similar result would not have been obtained by chance alone.

simple adaptive filtering   One of several variations of ADAPTIVE FILTERING.

simple average   Another name for the average or arithmetic mean.

simple regression   Regression with only one independent variable.

simulation   A trial run of a mathematical model, using some method of approximating a real-life situation.

single smoothed value (SSV)   In exponential smoothing, if the data show a significant trend, it is necessary to apply the exponential smoothing operation twice. The first time, you smooth the data points and the results are called single smoothed values. The second time, you smooth the single smoothed values themselves. The results of the second operation are called double smoothed values.

slope   In the graph of a straight line, the slope is the angle at which the line intercepts the X axis. In the equation of that line, the "slope" is the regression coefficient b.

slope model   *See* TREND MODEL.

SMA   Abbreviation for SEASONAL MOVING AVERAGE.

smoothing   Another word for finding the average of some numbers, but it is used in somewhat different contexts. Often it applies to a weighted average, as in exponential smoothing.

smoothing constant   The constant used in exponential smoothing, usually represented as alpha (α).

spectral analysis   A method of data analysis based on the frequency with which certain outcomes are observed.

Spencer's weighted moving average   A seasonal adjustment method that is used in various forecasting models, including Census II.

spline   A smoothing technique used to connect points in a graph.

SSV   Abbreviation for SINGLE SMOOTHED VALUE.

standard deviation   A statistic commonly used as a measure of dispersion; an estimator of the square root of the population variance. The formula is given in chapter 3.

standard error   Standard deviation.

standard error of the estimate (SEE)   In a regression model, the difference between the actual outcome and the forecast value.

stationarity   The absence of any significant trend or cyclic pattern in a set of data. Horizontal data (also known as stationary or level data) are said to exhibit stationarity.

statistics   A branch of applied mathematics which deals with techniques for collecting, analyzing, and drawing conclusions from data.

stepwise multiple regression   A method of multiple regression in which the program enters the independent variables into the model one at a time, beginning with the one that has the most explanatory value.

stepwise selection   Another name for stepwise multiple regression.

stochastic model   In nontechnical terms, a mathematical model that includes an error term.

stockout   The condition that occurs when an item is out of stock and must be back-ordered.

stratification   A method of drawing a sample by first dividing a population into several different groups (strata). These groups could include different geographic areas, age groups, or income levels, for example.

Student's t test   A common statistical test that is used to determine whether the means (averages) of two samples are significantly different or not. It can also be used to test the significance of the a and b parameters in regression. (The name of the test does not imply that it should be used only by students. *Student* was the pen name under which a statistician published the article in which he described this test.)

surrogate data   Another name for analogous data.

systematic sample   A sampling procedure that draws every nth unit from a population (such as every tenth or every fiftieth unit).

technological forecasting   A judgmental forecasting method based on considerations of current and projected trends in technology.

Theil's U coefficient   A statistical test often used to measure forecast accuracy.

time horizon   The length of time in the future for which a forecast is prepared. Usually classified as short-term, intermediate, and long-term, but the definitions vary.

time series   Any series of data points collected at uniform intervals over time.

time series analysis   Any mathematical method for analyzing time series data.

time series regression analysis   Regression analysis as applied to time series data.

tracking signal   A procedure for keeping track of forecasts, by determining whether they are consistently higher or lower than actual sales. If they are, then a tracking signal trip results.

tradeoff   In business forecasting, this word often is used to mean a compromise between two mutually exclusive goals. For example, if you want to ensure a service level of 99% but you can't afford to have that much money tied up in inventory, you might settle for a 95% service level instead.

transfer function model   A type of MARMA model that can be represented as a single equation.

transformation *See* DATA TRANSFORMATION.

trend The long-term tendency of a series of data points, such as a time series.

trend analysis A simple regression model in which time is the independent variable. A form of time series analysis.

trend impact analysis A computer-aided curve-fitting technique sometimes used in judgmental forecasting. The method enables the user to specify certain factors that might alter an established trend in some data, and to define probabilities for each of them. The program determines how each factor would influence the trend.

trend line A regression line in which the independent (*X*) variable is time. Thus a trend line is the graph of a time series model.

trending data Often called "trend data," time series data that shows a statistically significant trend or pattern of change over time.

trend-seasonal data Time series data that includes both trending and seasonal patterns.

trip A demand filter is designed to "catch" bad forecasts and alert the user to their presence, just as a burglar might trip an alarm system. Therefore, the word trip is used in the same sense with respect to demand filters.

triple smoothed value (TSV) The results of triple exponential smoothing are called triple smoothed values.

trough A low point on a graph of cyclic or seasonal data.

TSV Abbreviation for TRIPLE SMOOTHED VALUE.

t test *See* STUDENT'S T TEST.

turning point A point in a graph where a trend changes direction.

U statistic Another name for THEIL'S U [COEFFICIENT].

uncertainty Another name for random error.

univariate regression A regression model in which there is one independent (*X*) variable and one dependent (*Y*) variable.

universe Another name for a population, in the statistical sense.

variable In math, a symbol that represents some quantity of interest. For example, in a time series problem, you might use a variable called *X* to represent the months of the year. This variable could take on the numeric values 1 through 12. In computer programming, a variable is a storage location in the computer's memory which contains a value or a list of values.

variance In business, any sort of difference or variation. Sometimes it refers to a mistake in a manufacturing process which results in a product that does not meet specifications. In statistics, however, it is a measure of the amount of variability in a population.

VARMA Abbreviation for vector ARMA; same thing as MARMA.

V-mask A test sometimes used in forecast monitoring.

vector A matrix that has only one row or one column of numbers.

waiting line model Another name for a queuing model.

Weibull distribution A mathematical distribution often useful in development of models for predicting product failure rates.

weight   The relative importance assigned to one of several variables in a model, or to one of several successive values of the same variable. Usually it is expressed as a multiplier.

weighted average   An average calculated from weighted data, so that some of the data values influence the result more than others.

white noise   Another name for random error or noise.

Wilks' Lambda   In discriminant analysis, a test determine how well the model is predicting group membership. A smaller value of Wilks' Lambda generally indicates a better model.

Winters method   A method of exponential smoothing designed to accommodate seasonal and trend patterns in data.

working stock   Another name for cycle stock.

X-11   *See* CENSUS X-11.

X variable   The independent variable in a standard regression model.

Y intercept   On the graph of a regression line, the point at which the line crosses the Y axis.

Y variable   The dependent variable in a standard regression model.

zero-one variable   Another name for a DUMMY VARIABLE, which can take on only the values 0 and 1.

Z-score   A data value that has been normalized by subtracting the mean and dividing the difference by the standard deviation. The resulting number tells you that the original data value is above or below the mean by Z standard deviations.

Bibliography

Achen, C. H. "Interpreting and Using Regression." *Quantitative Applications in the Social Sciences*, Vol. 29 (1982).

Anderson, O. D., and M. R. Perryman, "Applied Time Series Analysis" (Proceedings of the International Conference Held at Houston, Texas, August 1981). Amsterdam: North-Holland Publishing Company, 1982.

Armstrong, J. S. *Long-Range Forecasting: From Crystal Ball to Computer.* New York: John Wiley & Sons, 1985.

Bails, D. G., and L. C. Peppers, *Business Fluctuations: Forecasting Techniques and Applications.* Englewood Cliffs, NJ: Prentice-Hall, Inc., 1982.

Baxter, B. S. "Forecasting Sales and Production of Synthetic Organic Chemicals With Microcomputers," (M.S. Thesis, University of Arkansas, 1987).

Beaumont, C., E. Mahmoud and V. E. McGee. Microcomputer Forecasting Software: A Survey. *Journal of Forecasting* 4(1985):305-311.

Berry, W. D., and S. Feldman, *Multiple Regression in Practice: Quantitative Applications in the Social Sciences*, Vol. 50. Beverly Hills: Sage Publications, 1985.

Box, G. E. P., and G. M. Jenkins. *Time-Series Analysis.* San Francisco: Holden-Day, 1976.

Brown, R. G. *Statistical Forecasting for Inventory Control.* New York: McGraw-Hill, 1959.

Carbone, R., R. Bilongo, P. Piat-Corson and S. Nadeau, "AEP Filtering." Chapter 6 in *The Forecasting Accuracy of Major Time Series Methods*, by Makridakis, S., et al. New York: John Wiley & Sons, 1984.

Chalmer, B. *Understanding Statistics.* New York: Marcel Dekker, Inc., 1987.

Chambers, J. C., S. K. Mullick, and D. D. Smith, *An Executive's Guide to Forecasting.* New York: John Wiley & Sons, 1974.

Chatfield, C., and D. L. Prothero, "Box-Jenkins Seasonal Forecasting Problems in a Case Study." *Journal of the Royal Statistical Society*: Series A, 136(1973):295-352.

Chow, G. C. "Tests of Equality Between Sets of Coefficients in Two Linear Regressions." *Econometrica* 28(1960):591-605.

Draper, N. R., and H. Smith, *Applied Regression Analysis*. New York: John Wiley & Sons, (1966).

Enrick, N. L. *Market and Sales Forecasting: A Quantitative Approach*. Huntington, New York: Robert E. Krieger Publishing Company, 1979.

Fildes, R., and S. Howell, "On Selecting a Forecasting Model." In *Forecasting. Studies in the Management Sciences*, edited by Makridakis, S., and S. C. Wheelwright, vol. 12: 297-312 Amsterdam: North-Holland Publishing Company, 1979.

Gardner, E. S., Jr. "Automatic Monitoring of Forecast Errors." *Journal of Forecasting* 2(1983):1-21.

_____. "Exponential Smoothing—The State of the Art: Extrapolative Methods." *Journal of Forecasting* 4(1985):1-38.

Harvey, A. C. "A Unified View of Statistical Forecasting." *Journal of Forecasting* 3(1984):245-275.

Hill, G., and R. Fildes, "The Accuracy of Extrapolation Methods: An Automatic Box-Jenkins Package (SIFT)." *Journal of Forecasting* 3(1984):319-323.

Hoff, J. C. *A Practical Guide to Box-Jenkins Forecasting*. Belmont, CA: Lifetime Learning Publications, 1983.

Huff, D. *How to Lie With Statistics*. New York: W. W. Norton, 1954.

Jenkins, G. M., and A. S. Alavi, "Some Aspects of Modelling and Forecasting Multivariate Time Series." *Journal of Time Series Analysis* 2(1981):1-47.

Koehler, A. B., and E. S. Murphree, "A comparison of the AIC and BIC on Empirical Data." Paper presented at the Sixth International Symposium on Forecasting, Paris, 1986.

Kress, G. *Practical Techniques of Business Forecasting: Fundamentals and Applications for Marketing, Production, and Financial Managers*. Westport, CT: Quorum Books, 1985.

Levenbach, H., and J. P. Cleary. *The Beginning Forecaster: The Forecasting Process Through Data Analysis*. Belmont, CA: Lifetime Learning Publications, 1981.

Lewis, C. D. *Industrial and Business Forecasting Methods*. London: Butterworth Scientific, 1982.

Lewis-Beck, M. S. *Applied Regression: An Introduction: Quantitative Applications in the Social Sciences*, Vol. 22. Beverly Hills: Sage Publications, 1980.

Libert, G. "The M-Competition With a Fully Automatic Box-Jenkins Procedure." *Journal of Forecasting* 3(1984):325-328.

Mabert, V. A. "Statistical Versus Sales Force-Executive Opinion Short Range Forecasts: A Time Series Analysis Case Study." Paper No. 487, Institute for Research in the Behavioral, Economic, and Management Sciences, Purdue University, 1974.

Mahmoud, E. "Accuracy in Forecasting: A Survey." *Journal of Forecasting* 3(1984):139-159.

Mahmoud, E., G. Rice, V. E. McGee, and C. Beaumont. "Mainframe Specific-Purpose Forecasting Software: A Survey." *Journal of Forecasting* 55(1986):75-83.

_____. 1986. Mainframe Multipurpose Forecasting Software: A Survey. Journal of Forecasting 5(2):127-137.

Makridakis, S., A. Anderson, R. Carbone, R. Fildes, M. Hibon, R. Lewandowski, J. Newton, E. Parzen, and R. Winkler. *The Forecasting Accuracy of Major Time Series Methods.* New York: John Wiley & Sons, 1984.

Makridakis, S., and S. C. Wheelwright. *Interactive Forecasting.* Edited by C. Doerr. Palo Alto, CA: The Scientific Press, 1974.

Forecasting: Studies in the Management Sciences, Volume 12. Edited by S. Makridakis and S. C. Wheelwright. Amsterdam: North-Holland Publishing Company, 1979.

Makridakis, S., and S. C. Wheelwright. *The Handbook of Forecasting: A Manager's Guide.* New York: John Wiley & Sons, 1982.

Marquardt, D. W. An algorithm for least squares estimation of nonlinear parameters. *Journal of the Society of Industrial and Applied Mathematics* 11(1963):431-441.

McLaughlin, R. L. Forecasting Models: Sophisticated or Naive? *Journal of Forecasting* 2(1983):274-276.

Mehra, R. K. "Kalman Filters and Their Appications to Forecasting." In *Forecasting. Studies in the Management Sciences.* Edited by S. Makridakis, and S. C. Wheelwright. Volume 12: 75-94. Amsterdam: North-Holland Publishing Company, 1979.

Mentzer, J. T. and J. E. Cox, Jr. "Familiarity, Application, and Performance of Sales Forecasting Techniques." *Journal of Forecasting* 3(1984):27-36.

Newbold, P. "Time-Series Model Building and Forecasting: A Survey." In *Forecasting. Studies in the Management Sciences.* Edited by S. Makridakis, and S. C. Wheelwright. Volume 12: 59-74. Amsterdam: North-Holland Publishing Company, 1979.

Ostrom, C. W., Jr. *Time Series Analysis: Regression Techniques. Quantitative Applications in the Social Sciences,* vol. 9. Beverly Hills: Sage Publications, 1978.

Parzen, E. "ARARMA Models for Time Series Analysis and Forecasting." *Journal of Forecasting* 1(1982): 66-82.

Plossl, G. W. "Getting the Most From Forecasts." Paper presented at the International Conference of the American Production and Inventory Control Society, 1972.

Roberts, H. V. "Selection of Statistical Software for Micros." *Computers and the Social Sciences* 2(1986):65-68.

Sackman, H. *Delphi Critique: Expert Opinion, Forecasting, and Group Process.* Lexington, MA: D.C. Heath, 1975.

Sartorius, L. C., and N. C. Mohn. "Sales Forecasting Models: A Diagnostic Approach." Research Monograph No. 69, (1976), Georgia State University, 239-241.

Snedecor, G. W., and W. G. Cochran. *Statistical Methods.* 6th ed. Ames, Iowa: Iowa State University Press, 1967.

Steece, B. "Evaluation of Forecasts." In *The Handbook of Forecasting: A Manager's Guide*. Edited by S. Makridakis, and S. C. Wheelwright, New York: John Wiley & Sons, 1982.

Terry, L. M., and W. R. Terry. "A Multiple Time Series Analysis of Cotton-Polyester Market Competition." Edited by O. D. Anderson, and M. R. Perryman. In *Applied Time Series Analysis: Proceedings of the International Conference Held at Houston, Texas, August 1981*. Amsterdam: North-Holland Publishing Company, 1982.

Wheelwright, S. C., and D. Clarke. "Corporate Forecasting: Promise and Reality." *Harvard Business Review*, November-December, 1976.

Wheelwright, S. C., and S. Makridakis. *Forecasting Methods for Management*. New York: John Wiley, 1985.

White, H. R. 1984. *Sales Forecasting: Timesaving and Profit-Making Strategies That Work*. Glenview, Illinois: Scott, Foresman and Company, 1984.

Woolsey, R. E. D., and H. F. Swanson. *Operations Research for Immediate Application: A Quick and Dirty Manual*. New York: Harper and Row, 1975.

Index

About the Authors

Joan Callahan Compton holds the position of Senior Scientist for MBC Applied Environmental Sciences in Costa Mesa, California. She is a research associate of the University of Georgia and has also taught at the University of Arizona, where she received her doctorate in 1976. This is her third book.

Steve Compton is employed as Senior Quality Engineer for Bear Medical Systems in Riverside, California. He has eleven years of experience in software engineering, with emphasis on mathematical and statistical applications. He is presently writing a book on software configuration management.